THE TASTE OF OUR TIME

Collection planned and directed by

ALBERT SKIRA

BIOGRAPHICAL AND CRITICAL STUDY

BY

JACQUES LASSAIGNE

TRANSLATED BY STUART GILBERT

MIRÓ

Title page:
Woman, Bird, Star (detail), 1942.
Private Collection, Paris.

*

Distributed by Crown Publishers, Inc.
419 Park Avenue South, New York, N.Y. 10016

© 1963 by Editions d'Art Albert Skira, Geneva
Library of Congress Catalog Card Number: 63-8983
New edition 1972

CHRONOLOGICAL SURVEY

1893 Birth of Joan Miró Ferra, April 20, at Barcelona.

1896 Birth of André Masson.

1898 Birth of René Magritte.

1900 Birth of Yves Tanguy.

1901 Birth of Alberto Giacometti.

1905-1906 First drawings from nature, at Cornudella, Prades and in the countryside near Palma (Majorca).

1907 Attends a commercial school and the La Lonja School of Fine Arts, where he studies under Modesto Urgell and José Pasco.

1910 Works as a clerk in a drugstore.

1911 Falls seriously ill. Recuperates in the house his parents have just bought at Montroig.

1912 Enrolls in the art academy of Francisco Gali, where he meets E. C. Ricart and Llorens Artigas.

1912 Exhibition of Impressionist, Fauve and Cubist works at the Dalmau Gallery, Barcelona.

1915 Shares his first studio with Ricart, at 51 Baja San Pedro, near Barcelona Cathedral. Draws from the nude at the San Lluch Club, where he meets Joan Prats and Rafols. Paints his first still lifes.

1916 Encouraged by Dalmau, who promises to exhibit his work, he paints landscapes at Montroig. Reads poems by Apollinaire and Reverdy in the review Nord-Sud.

1916 Vollard organizes a large exhibition of French art at Barcelona.

1917 Paints landscapes at Ciurana, Prades, Montroig and Cambrils. First portraits.

1917 Picabia launches the Dada review "391" at Barcelona.

1918 First exhibition at the Dalmau Gallery, prefaced by a calligram by Junoy. Joins the group known as the "Agrupación Courbet," led by Artigas. Paints "detailist" landscapes at Montroig.

1919 Meets Maurice Raynal. First trip to Paris, where he calls on Picasso.

1920 From now on he spends the winter in Paris and the summer at Montroig. In Paris he meets Reverdy, Tzara, and Max Jacob, who introduces him to André Masson. Masson moves into the studio next door to Miró's at 45 Rue Blomet. Large still lifes.

1920 Dada demonstrations in Paris.

1921 Miró's first one-man show in Paris (Galerie La Licorne), prefaced by Maurice Raynal. Begins "The Farm," finished in 1922.

1922 Around Masson and Miró a group of young writers forms the so-called Rue Blomet Group.

1923 Exhibits with the Catalan painters at the Salon d'Automne. Begins "The Tilled Field" at Montroig.

1924 Paints "The Harlequin's Carnival." Meets Aragon, Breton and Eluard. Takes part in the activities of the surrealist group.

1925 Miró Exhibition at the Galerie Pierre, prefaced by Benjamin Péret. Takes part in the Surrealist Exhibition at the same gallery. Dream paintings (1925-1927).

1925 First exhibition of the surrealist painters at the Galerie Pierre, Paris, with Arp, Chirico, Ernst, Klee, Man Ray, Masson, Miró, Picasso and Pierre Roy.

1926 Collaborates with Max Ernst on sets for "Romeo and Juliet" (Ballets Russes). Paints "Imaginary Landscapes" at Montroig (1926-1927).

1926 Opening of the Surrealist Gallery, Rue Jacques Callot, Paris. Calder in Paris. Launching of the "Cahiers d'Art."

1927 Moves to the Cité des Fusains, Rue Tourlaque, where Arp, Ernst, Eluard and Magritte also live.

1927 Tanguy, Ernst and Arp exhibitions in Paris.

1928 Trip to Holland. Back in Paris, he paints his "Dutch Interiors" inspired by pictures in the Rijksmuseum, Amsterdam. Miró Exhibition at the Galerie Bernheim organized by Pierre Loeb. First papiers collés and collages.

1928 André Breton publishes "Le Surréalisme et la Peinture." At Dinard Picasso paints "Bathers."

1929 "Imaginary Portraits" after several Old Master paintings. Marries Pilar Juncosa at Palma (Majorca), October 12. Moves to 3 Rue François Mouthon, Paris.

1929 Breton publishes the Second Surrealist Manifesto. "Un Chien Andalou," motion picture by Bunuel and Dali.

1930 Exhibits papiers collés at the Galerie Pierre and takes part in an exhibition of collages at the Galerie Goemans. First one-man show in New York at the Valentin Gallery.

1930 Publication of "Le Surréalisme au service de la révolution."

1931 Birth of his daughter Dolores at Barcelona, July 17. Exhibits "object-sculptures" at the Galerie Pierre, Paris, and paintings at the Arts Club of Chicago.

1931 Object-sculptures by Giacometti.

1932 Sets, costumes and curtain for Massine's ballet "Jeux d'Enfants," music by Bizet. Small paintings on wood. Exhibitions at the Galerie Pierre, Paris, and the Pierre Matisse Gallery, New York, which henceforth represents Miró in the United States and holds regular showings of his work. Exhibits with the Surrealists at the Salon des Surindépendants in Paris.

1932 Founding of the Abstraction-Creation group in Paris.

1933 Miró Exhibition at the Galerie Bernheim, Paris (collage drawings and large paintings after collages).

1933 Albert Skira launches the review "Minotaure." The Berlin Bauhaus closes down. Klee returns to Switzerland and Kandinsky moves to Paris.

1934 Tapestry cartoons for Madame Cuttoli. Paintings on sandpaper. Large pastels on velvet-surface paper, initiating his so-called Wild Period ("période sauvage").

1935 Takes part in the Surrealist Exhibition at Tenerife (Canary Islands). Makes several long stays in Catalonia. "Wild" paintings on cardboard.

1936 Paintings on copper and on masonite. Leaves Spain (not to return until 1940) for Paris and takes rooms in a Montparnasse hotel (Rue Jules Chaplain).

1936 Assassination of Calvo Sotelo on July 13. General Franco lands at Tetuan. Outbreak of the Spanish Civil War. Surrealist Exhibition in London.

1937 Draws from the nude at the Académie de la Grande-Chaumière. Paints "Still Life with an Old Shoe." Moves to the Boulevard Blanqui. Large mural painting on celotex, "The Reaper," for the Spanish Pavilion at the Paris World's Fair. Takes part in the exhibition "L'Art International Indépendant" organized by Zervos at the Musée du Jeu de Paume. Paintings on celotex. Many watercolors and gouaches. Self-portrait.

1937 Nazi campaign against "degenerate" art in Germany.

1938 Does some etchings in Marcoussis' studio. Spends the summer at Varengeville (Normandy) with the architect Nelson.

1938 International Surrealist Exhibition in Paris (Galerie des Beaux-Arts).

1939 Takes a house at Varengeville (Clos des Sansonnets). Series of paintings on the theme of "A Bird in Flight above the Plain." Paintings on burlap.

1939 Outbreak of the Second World War.

1940 Begins the "Constellations." On May 20, during the German invasion of France, he returns to Paris and catches the last train for Barcelona, where he is welcomed by his friend Prats. Settles temporarily at Palma de Mallorca.

1940 International Surrealist Exhibition in Mexico City.

1941 Finishes the "Constellations" at Palma and Montroig. First retrospective exhibition at the Museum of Modern Art, New York, organized by J. J. Sweeney, whose catalogue contains the first monograph on Miró.

1941 Breton, Ernst and Chagall arrive in the United States, where Tanguy is already living. Masson joins them in 1942.

1942 Miró moves back to Barcelona.

1944 Death of his mother. Lithographs and first ceramics in collaboration with Artigas.

1944 Death of Kandinsky in Paris.

1945 "Constellations" and first ceramics exhibited at the Pierre Matisse Gallery, New York.

1947 First trip to the United States. Stays in New York and works on a mural painting for the restaurant of a Cincinnati hotel. Does etchings in Hayter's Atelier 17.

1947 International Surrealist Exhibition ("Le Surréalisme en 1947") at the Galerie Maeght, Paris.

1948 Returns to Paris. At the Galerie Maeght (which henceforth represents him in France) he exhibits 88 recent works. Engravings and lithographs.

1948 The Venice Biennale resumes its activities: prizes awarded to Braque for painting, to Henry Moore for sculpture, to Chagall for engraving.

1949 Exhibition in Barcelona of early works belonging to Catalan collectors. Retrospectives at the Kunsthalle, Bern, and the Kunsthalle, Basel.

1950 Moves back to Barcelona, taking an apartment in the Calle Folgarolas while keeping his old studio in the Pasaje del Credito. First woodcuts for a book published in Barcelona. Mural painting for Harvard University. Exhibition at the Galerie Maeght.

1951 First São Paulo Biennale.

1952 Death of Paul Eluard.

1953 Commemorative exhibition at the Galerie Maeght for the artist's sixtieth birthday.

1954 Traveling exhibition in Germany: Krefeld, Stuttgart, Berlin. Guest of honor at the Italian pavilion of the Venice Biennale, where he exhibits paintings and sculptures, his lithographs being shown at the Spanish Pavilion. Awarded first prize for engraving.

1954 At the Venice Biennale, Max Ernst awarded first prize for painting, Zadkine for sculpture.
Death of Maurice Raynal.

1955 In collaboration with Artigas, Miró now devotes himself entirely to ceramics (until 1959).

1955 Death of Tanguy. First Documenta Exhibition at Kassel.

1956 Exhibits ceramics at the Galerie Maeght, Paris, and the Pierre Matisse Gallery, New York. Large-scale retrospective exhibition held successively at the Palais des Beaux-Arts, Brussels, the Municipal Museum, Amsterdam, and the Kunsthalle, Basel. Leaves Barcelona and settles for good at Palma de Mallorca, where the architect J. L. Sert builds him the "big studio" he had dreamt of for years.

1957 Begins work on two ceramic murals for the new Unesco Building in Paris; finishes them in 1958. Traveling exhibition of his complete graphic work at Krefeld, Berlin, Munich, Cologne, Hanover and Hamburg.

1958 Takes part in the "Fifty Years of Modern Art" exhibition at the Brussels World's Fair. Exhibits his "peintures sauvages" (1934-1953) at the Pierre Matisse Gallery, New York. 80 woodcut illustrations for Paul Eluard's poem "A toute épreuve."

1959 Second visit to the United States for a large-scale retrospective exhibition of his work at the Museum of Modern Art, New York, and the Los Angeles Museum.
Awarded the Guggenheim Prize for his Unesco murals. Begins painting again.

1959 Second Documenta Exhibition at Kassel.

1960 In collaboration with Artigas, he executes a ceramic mural for Harvard University, exhibited in 1961 at the Sala Gaspar, Barcelona, the Galerie Maeght, Paris, and the Guggenheim Museum, New York.

1961 Mural paintings. Double exhibition of recent paintings at the Galerie Maeght. Exhibition of his graphic work and ceramics at the Musée de l'Athénée, Geneva. Third trip to the United States.

1962 Large-scale retrospective exhibition at the Musée d'Art Moderne, Paris.

1964 Inauguration at Saint-Paul de Vence (French Riviera) of the Maeght foundation and its Labyrinth decorated with sculptures and ceramics by Miró. One room is devoted to a permanent exhibition of his work. Takes part in Documenta III, Kassel.

1966 Visits Japan for his large retrospective in Tokyo and Kyoto.

1967 Awarded the Carnegie Prize for painting. His large ceramic mural, made in collaboration with Artigas, inaugurated at the Solomon R. Guggenheim Museum, New York.

1968 Large retrospectives at the Maeght Foundation and in Barcelona.

1969 "Miró Otro" exhibition at the House of Architects in Barcelona, where he paints a vast mural which, when the exhibition is over, he completely obliterates.

1970 Miró and Artigas execute a ceramic mural measuring 165 by 32 feet for Barcelona airport.

INTRODUCTION

To discard inherited traditions and regain the pristine innocence and spontaneity of the creative act—such is one of
the most cherished ideals of the vanguard artist today in the old
civilizations of the West. But the goal is only to be reached by
way of long and arduous preparation, of patient research and
an intense withdrawal into himself, until at last, all barriers down,
the artist breaks through into the light, weaving his arabesques,
letting his color run free and bringing the picture surface to
vivid life in a dazzling flash of inspiration.

Miró's work, more than any other in the whole field of
modern art, embodies the fruits of this conquest of innocence,
of youth, of joyous freedom.

Beginning, over forty years ago, with an objective interpretation of village scenes and Spanish peasant life, Miró defined
the elements of this world with precision but clad them in deli-
cate, pearly colors and invested them with a lyrical, almost
Oriental charm. Soon, however, after coming in contact with
Dada and Surrealism, he broke down and dissociated these
elements, leaving each to be deciphered and identified in a
maze of metamorphoses and simplifications. Instead of synthe-

sizing the various aspects of an object, he seizes on and isolates what for him is its most characteristic trait—generally the one we least expect. In his hands the sign is reinvested with its primordial function and lives a life of its own, quite apart from the qualities we associate with it in real life. Miró thus arrives at archetypal figurations of women, birds and stars, and with new hieroglyphs creates a language of his own.

Miró's technical innovations have the same arresting originality and interest. He does not hesitate to incorporate "foreign bodies," unusual materials, in his pictures and to add passages in relief emphasizing depth. He has succeeded in breaking down the barriers between techniques and ingeniously combining them, as when he uses the granulations of canvas and frayed edges of burlap to implement effects of scumbled color; or, splashing liquids on to cardboard or paper, conjures up new, fascinating forms from their meanders. Moreover he has produced in collaboration with Artigas, that prince of potters, a number of ceramics, an art on which, at various stages of his career, he has concentrated his activity for several years running, building up a whole world of fantastic, hybrid creatures, "object-sculptures" and glazed terracottas. These experiences have enabled him both to enrich his repertory of forms and to give an unsurpassed depth and brilliance to his colors. Such indeed is their potency and impact that they never fail to give the spectator "that blow in the face which sweeps him off his feet before he can begin to collect his thoughts," which Miró described as one of his objectives in his talk with Georges Duthuit, reproduced *in extenso* at a later page.

Miró's art is full of a salutary humor and high spirits. His poetic vision enables him to sublimate even the humblest "supports," and to invent gay, life-enhancing forms which contain the makings of a new mythology befitting the world-view of modern man.

JOAN MIRÓ

CIURANA, 1917. JOAQUIM GOMIS COLLECTION, BARCELONA.

THE FORMATIVE YEARS

"...a singular emotion that things of nature
in their place are unable to provoke."

PIERRE REVERDY

JOAN MIRÓ was born in 1893 at Barcelona where his parents
then were living in a rather ugly nineteenth-century house
on the Pasaje del Credito, in the heart of the old town. He spent
his youth in these uninspiring surroundings and it was here
that his mother died. The artist kept his parents' apartment
and the studio he had installed in a low-roofed room on the
upper floor until 1956. There he often worked, particularly
when giving the finishing touches to pictures begun elsewhere.
This little world was exactly what he needed; in it he felt secure
from outside interference and ran no risk of being distracted
from his work.

His father, Miguel Miró, a goldsmith and watchmaker, was
the son of a blacksmith hailing from Cornudella, a large
town in the Sierra de Montsant in the province of Tarragona.
After settling in the small near-by town of Reus (Gaudi's
hometown), he had moved to Barcelona, where he prospered
in his business and was much looked up to. At the Oromi shoe-
store in the Pasaje he made the acquaintance of Dolorès Ferra,
daughter of the owner, and she became his wife. Miguel Miró
was a conscientious craftsman wholly absorbed in his work,

and there was little gaiety in the atmosphere. Miró respected his father and took care not to offend the susceptibilities of that worthy, if narrow-minded man, but it was to his mother only that he looked for understanding and affection. Keenly as he suffered from the depressing ambience of his home life, he kept his feelings in check and, though inwardly seething with revolt, was careful to avoid conflicts which would merely cause distress and lead to nothing. Here we have perhaps the origin of Miró's tenacity of purpose, his patience, his occasional moods of taciturnity. Loyal to his parents in all that concerned his conduct, he nursed his yearnings to break free in silence.

From his earliest years he had a taste for drawing, and brought to it the constant diligence of an industrious craftsman. He loathed school, but happily there was a drawing course and at this he worked "with a high seriousness, as if performing a religious rite." In some of these early efforts he displayed an incredible clumsiness, but soon he learnt instinctively to tackle his problems piecemeal, isolate objects and firmly to record their outlines. When he started drawing from nature in the neighborhood of Cornudella and in Majorca (where he often spent his holidays), he made a point of simplifying the object and stripping the contour of every superfluity, so as to give clearer definition to his line. After making sketches of architectural features that had caught his eye—bridges and ancient churches and the like—he already showed much skill in disposing them in appropriate settings: a village or a stretch of country. Sometimes too he lingers on a detail, scanning and recording each particularity with extreme precision; often a mere tuft of grass or a bird in the sky is given an abnormal prominence.

As he was making little headway in high school he was sent in 1907 to a commercial school and also given permission to attend classes at the La Lonja School of Fine Arts which specialized in turning out competent practitioners of the decorative arts and where originality was discouraged. Miró adapted himself as best he could to these rather irksome conditions, and he was fortunate in having two perceptive teachers, Modesto Urgell and José Pasco. Recognizing the boy's shut-in disposition, Urgell encouraged him to think things out for himself and to practise a sensitive approach to nature. Pasco, a more dynamic teacher, was all for reviving the spirit of primitive Catalan art, while incorporating in it modern discoveries and techniques. Stimulated by his contacts with this teacher, Miró made rapid progress, became alive to the possibilities of color and tried his hand at original stylizations.

His three years' studies at the commercial school led to nothing and he accepted the post of clerk in a drugstore. Here he was overworked to such a point that he fell seriously ill. His parents sent him to the country to recuperate, at the farm they had recently bought at Montroig, just below Cornudella, on the outskirts of the plain reaching to the sea. This was not only a welcome respite but the beginning of a lifelong attachment to this secluded village.

Montroig, "the red mountain," so named after the color of the cliffs overhanging the village (most famous being the spur of La Roca on which stands the Monastery of San Rámon), which have been hollowed out and molded by wind, rain and frost, was henceforth to be one of the focal points of the painter's life: at once a place of refuge and an unfailing source of inspiration. The other focal point alternated between Barcelona and Paris (or, on occasion, Varengeville and New York). It was at Montroig that he had once regained his health, and every time he went there he could count on a new lease of energy and inspiration. Except during the Spanish Civil War, the years were few when he did not return to Montroig to replenish his creative vigor. In the farm, a rustic oasis slightly off the beaten track, with its light yet copious vegetation, kept in trim control by skillful husbandry, he found the balanced rhythm to which he constantly aspired and which indeed was fundamental to his art.

Restored to health and assured of his vocation, he at last succeeded in persuading his parents to let him follow his bent and devote himself exclusively to painting. He began by enrolling in the Academy Gali in Barcelona. Francisco Gali was a conscientious artist who played an active part in the life of Barcelona where he had founded a "free" academy in which the experimental art of contemporary foreign painters provided a corrective to the official curriculum. He inculcated in his pupils a taste for literature and music, encouraged them to discuss general ideas, and stimulated each to get the best out of himself and strike out on personal lines. To Miró he suggested an unusual method of acquiring a feeling for form (in which he was then deficient) and made him draw objects by the sense of touch alone, without looking at them. And very soon Miró developed a gift for plastic form and modeling that stood him in good stead in his painting. In the Academy Gali, Miró made the acquaintance of other artists, among them E.C. Ricart, with whom in 1915 he shared a studio near the cathedral, at 51 Baja San Pedro; and also met Llorens Artigas with whom he was later to collaborate in a series of ceramics. On leaving the Academy, so as to be able to work from models, he often visited the San Lluch Club which occupied what had been the premises of the "Quatre Gats" Cabaret and subsequently became a marionette theater. It was there he met J.F. Rafols and Joan Prats who was to be his closest friend.

Miró's œuvre has always had a tendency to run in cycles. None of his achievements stands alone; each represents a more or less fully realized way of feeling, thinking and conceiving. Incidents, emotional shocks may lead on occasion to drastic cleavages, but there is usually a certain time-lag in these changes;

THE BALCONY, 1917. GALERIE MAEGHT, PARIS.

moreover, almost every new development, abandoned for the nonce, is subsequently followed up, though sometimes reappearing under another guise. Thus all these works end up by throwing light on and complementing each other. Always fully conscious and coherent, Miró makes a point of carrying his ideas through to their logical conclusion. He produces sequences of pictures as complete as possible, while taking care never to repeat himself or to overwork a procedure. Thus he was from the very start. In an early group of still lifes (1915) we find depictions of the object in front view, with the line emphasized by violent color and sometimes slightly deviated by its impact. In 1916 the distortion becomes systematic and angular (Cubist works had been on view in Barcelona at the Dalmau Gallery since 1912). Corresponding to the distortion of the central object (e.g. a bottle or plate) are angles arbitrarily introduced into the setting, or modifying the structure of accessories (e.g. a table, a newspaper, a wall). Intricate in the earlier works, the composition becomes simpler; we have the climax of this tendency in 1917 in the still life called *Nord-Sud* (after the magazine that figures in it) whose finely balanced composition comprises isolated elements, evenly distributed on the picture surface and deriving their intensity from a note of pure color.

We find a similar process starting with the nudes of 1915, built of dark, sweeping curves stressing muscles and gestures, and leading to those of 1917, with their odd protrusions, which culminate in the *Standing Nude* of 1918 (Pierre Matisse Collection, New York), where the strongly modeled figure stands out against a curtain gayly patterned with flowers and birds.

In 1917 Miró embarked on a series of large portraits (nine had been made by 1919), which may be regarded as the first deliberate assertion of his personality. After two self-portraits he made likenesses of his painter friends, and of a young girl. Leaving out of account the second portrait and the *Young Girl*

(1919), with their somewhat superficial stylizations, we find in the other seven a remarkable uniformity in the means of expression now employed by Miró. The earliest is that of Vicente Nubiola in which the actual portrait occupies only half the canvas, the rest being taken up by a large still life of fruit, flowers and a *porrón* (Catalan jug). In the first self-portrait (Bragaline Collection, New York), in the portraits of Rafols (Schoenberg Collection, St. Louis) and the half-length of Ramón Sunyer, as in those of Ricart (Marx Collection, New York) and Juanita Obrador (Art Institute of Chicago)—these last are more complete and richly worked—we are struck by the prominence given the face, the bulging cheeks, bulbous nose and the curious thickening of the upper lip that determines the facial expression. Planes of strident color, green, yellow, mauve, enhanced with a little blue, are bound in thick black contour lines. In the portraits of Juanita and Ricart the face is assimilated to the garment (pyjama or dress) whose stripes of contrasting, iridescent hues form a color scheme reiterated in the model's features. These stripes create, moreover, a plangent rhythm imparting to the figure as a whole a majestic, strangely obsessive actuality. It stands out on a ground containing decorative elements sometimes of a symbolic order. Thus in the portrait of Ricart we see in the top left-hand corner a palette shaped like a boldly stylized face; in the portrait of Heriberto Casany (Bragaline Collection, New York) the picture of a motor-car hung on the wall, and in Ramón Sunyer's, the image of a flower serving as a goldsmith's model. Hence the names the pictures are sometimes given (not by Miró): "The Chauffeur," "Portrait of a Goldsmith."

In these works Miró solved, almost at his first attempt, the problem of portraiture. This direct confrontation with the living model was a valuable experience, and he quickly mastered the art of singling out the most significant traits; yet, though fully

PORTRAIT OF JUANITA OBRADOR, 1918.
JOSEPH WINTERBOTHAM COLLECTION, THE ART INSTITUTE OF CHICAGO.

◄   PORTRAIT OF E.C. RICART, 1917.
COLLECTION OF MR AND MRS SAMUEL A. MARX, NEW YORK.

individualized, his figures end up by having a certain family likeness and are in a sense synthetic. Meanwhile, however, Miró was exploring other, more accessible domains of art, and it was in landscape, above all, that he trained his hand and eye.

His yearly stays at Montroig and his trips to mountain villages, Prades and the ancient hamlet of Ciurana perched on a lofty crag, or to the near-by beach of Cambrils, provided a wide range of visual experience. The mountain landscapes of 1917 testify to a close observation of the interlocking planes formed by the cliffs beside the winding roads, above which sometimes rises a church or a group of huts. Here he found natural formations that may well have suggested the structure of his portraits. He often tends to "geometrize" the foreground planes by a liberal use of curves, ellipses or herring-bone patterns, symbols of irregularities of the terrain, the brushwood covering them, and clumps of bushes rising tier on tier along the mountainside. Here we have a basic stylization and the makings of a repertoire of elementary forms serving at once to body forth and to summarize a landscape. At the same time the colors become sparser and develop a significance independent of what they represent. The countryside around Montroig, with its river, bridge and stretches of level ground, did not lend itself so well to architectonic interpretation and Miró preferred to concentrate on isolated elements. In his depictions of the light-drenched port and beach of Cambrils, strewn with boats and tiny figures, their shadows lengthened by the sun, Miró is trying to discover and define characteristic signs for human beings and animals in a state of tension or in movement.

Some have spoken of a "Catalan Fauvism" apropos of these pictures. But the reminiscences of Fauve art (already of the past) are slight. Cubism, too, had found its way to Barcelona, but undoubtedly the art that most affected Miró at this early stage was that of the two great pathfinders, Cézanne and Van Gogh.

During the Great War Vollard organized a large-scale exhibition of French art in the Catalan capital and in it figured works by the Impressionists, Cézanne, the Nabis and Matisse. When Miró and his friends decided to form a group they placed it under the

Miro 6

THE FARM, 1921-1922. FORMER ERNEST HEMINGWAY COLLECTION, HAVANA.

aegis of Courbet, and the "Agrupación Courbet," led by
Artigas, was allotted a room in the municipal exhibition at
Barcelona in 1918 and 1919. Miró frequently visited the Dalmau
Gallery, a favorite rendezvous of foreign visitors, and here he

met Maurice Raynal and Francis Picabia. It was here, too, early in 1918, that he gave his first one-man show, for which José Maria Junoy composed a prefatory "calligram" in the manner of Apollinaire. Miró exhibited sixty-four paintings and drawings made in the last four years, but pride of place was given to the numerous works produced in 1917.

Miró learnt much from this encounter with the general public. One gets an impression that he felt slightly abashed at having thus "given himself away" by allowing free course to his natural exuberance and tendency to somewhat brutal methods of expression. Accordingly he resolved to tighten up his composition and to return to Montroig where in self-imposed isolation he could take stock of his means and adjust them to the need he now felt for greater concentration and precision. Thus began what Rafols named his "detailist" period.

In the course of a few months he made several landscapes in this new manner: *Kitchen Garden with Donkey* (Schapiro Collection, New York), *The Tilery* (Alsdorf Collection, Winnetka, Ill.), *The Rut* (Stern Collection, New York); these were followed up in the next year by *The Church and Village* (owned by the artist), *The Olive Grove* (Block Collection, Chicago). Then, in 1921-1922, came that magnificent work *The Farm* begun at Montroig, continued in Barcelona and finished in Paris. Miró describes his feelings towards nature in letters he wrote to friends at this time, interesting extracts from which figure in Jacques Dupin's excellent study (Cologne-Paris, 1961). Thus Miró writes to Rafols of "the joy of achieving in a landscape a perfect comprehension of a blade of grass... as beautiful as a tree or a mountain," and to Ricart he confesses that "what most of all interests me is the calligraphy of the tiles on a roof or that of a tree scanned leaf by leaf, branch by branch." Patiently, painstakingly, he records sometimes quite minute details which he has singled out and isolated, and integrates, as meaningful constituents, into the formal structure he is building up. Individualized and invested with a poetic grace peculiarly its own, each detail acquires a new resonance. Like the crystalline notes of an exquisite cantabile, every plant and every frond, their forms and colors rendered with elegant fidelity, plays an essential part in the mellifluous perfection of the whole. Yet we find no trace of effort in this meticulously executed composition, on which the limpid purity of sky and light confers an otherworldly beauty. Architectural elements such as the village in the background, above the stylized gardens, are treated with the naive precision of a Primitive.

This tendency to stylization was particularly marked in *The Olive Grove* whose structure is determined by abstract forms and the geometrical lay-out of the terrain with its formal strips of cultivation. But here, too, for the first time we find typically surrealist touches; for example, the way the roots of the row of vines in the foreground are brought up on to the surface. Two years later, in *The Farm*, this trend was carried a stage further. The farm animals, dead or living, are set forth in side-view, without regard to scale, in a sort of pictorial inventory. The contents of the barn are displayed, neatly aligned on shelves, and cracks in the wall are rendered with pitiless precision. All is static, except for the plants and tree, pervaded with a restless agitation: the swirling leafage of the corn, the eucalyptus with its gnarled trunk and yellowish branches ending abruptly in clusters of grey petals. And in this carefully contrived synthesis we have anticipations of the forms he was soon to call into being.

In the *Still Life with Rabbit* (Zumsteg Collection, Zurich) and the *Still Life with Toy Horse* (Miller Collection, Downington, Pa.) of 1920, Miró summarizes the data of visual experience in another manner. On a sloping plane he lays out elements treated with an extreme realism. A curious tension makes itself felt between their volumes and the grounds, including the

Miro 8

STILL LIFE WITH RABBIT, 1920. GUSTAV ZUMSTEG COLLECTION, ZURICH.

THE CARBIDE LAMP, 1922-1923.
COLLECTION, THE MUSEUM OF MODERN ART, NEW YORK. PURCHASE.

surface of the table (here Miró perhaps owed something to the decorative Cubism of Juan Gris). He now employs a method of organizing space and linking diverse objects with each other which, despite an underlying rhythm, gives an impression of arbitrariness. But Miró was quick to remedy this; in *Table with*

Glove (Museum of Modern Art) of 1921, the table is tilted almost vertically and only indispensable elements are included. They are represented without depth, all on the surface, enlarged to the point of having a monumental aspect and disposed in a slightly florid arabesque. The fine spareness he now aimed at was

THE FARMER'S WIFE, 1922-1923.
COLLECTION OF MRS ALEXINA DUCHAMP, NEW YORK.

achieved only in the three last works of this phase: *The Grill*, *The Carbide Lamp* and *The Ear of Grain* (Museum of Modern Art).

In *The Farmer's Wife* (Duchamp Collection, New York) Miró reverts to the figures of *The Farm*, but carries them a stage further, and all the picture elements are boldly schematized. The stove, the towel hanging on the wall have forms as strictly geometric as that of the plate in the foreground. Indeed the whole pictorial structure is determined by a system of near abstract lines. For example, the only use of the diagonally placed flue is to form the side of a triangle. Even the animals, though relatively lifelike, are given an hieratic aspect. The model for the woman was a *santon* (Provençal doll) and the body has undergone some startling distortions, the immense feet serving as a fulcrum to the entire composition. This foundational effect is reinforced by the folds of her garment and the line of white patches formed by the toes of her right foot. Though of moderate dimensions, *The Farmer's Wife* produces a truly monumental effect. The purely plastic structure, with its skillful use of low-pitched, saturated colors, notably variations of browns set off by passages of blue, is superbly realized.

It may seem strange that Miró should have persisted so long in exploring the possibilities of a vocabulary he had so thoroughly mastered, and in confining his field of visual experience to the little world of Montroig, though (as we shall see) his life had been given a new orientation for some four years. This was not the only occasion on which he made a point of testing out to the full the possibilities of a way of seeing and a technique he had provisionally adopted, and we have here another illustration of the high seriousness he brought to each successive phase of his artistic career. Moreover, this "Montroig period" was preparative to all he was to create in later years; thus there were good reasons for its long duration.

MATERNITY, 1924. ROLAND PENROSE COLLECTION, LONDON.

SURREALIST ENFRANCHISEMENT

"Miró may rank as the most surrealist of us all."

ANDRÉ BRETON

MIRO's first trip to Paris, in the spring of 1919, was motivated by his deep conviction that in the atmosphere of Barcelona an art like his could never thrive. The battle was being fought elsewhere and he was determined to take part in it. This first visit was purely "to spy out the land." Artigas, who had preceded him, welcomed him to Paris. Miró went to the Louvre (the first great museum he visited) and called on Picasso, with whose family he was acquainted. His famous compatriot not only showed much kindness and affection but bought the picture— the second self-portrait—he had brought with him.

In June Miró returned to Montroig and continued painting landscapes. The following winter saw him back in Paris where once again he was hard put to it to find a place to live in. Maurice Raynal introduced him to Reverdy and Tzara and he attended the first Dada demonstration in Paris. He spent the summer at Montroig working on large still lifes. Returning to Paris at the end of the year, he at last succeeded in finding accommodation and settled into the studio at 45, Rue Blomet of the sculptor Gargallo, who spent the winter in Barcelona teaching art, coming back to Paris every summer.

Now that he had solved the problem of where to live, Miró could devote his time to painting. His productions included the *Portrait of a Spanish Dancer* (acquired by Picasso) and two uncompromisingly schematic works: the *Spanish Dancer on a Black Ground* (Urvater Collection) and the *Standing Nude* of the Penrose Collection. He also made preparations for the one-man show at the Galerie La Licorne organized for him by Dalmau. This lasted from April 29 to May 14, 1921, and attracted little attention, despite a glowing preface to the catalogue by Maurice Raynal who spoke of "a splendid contribution to the art of the imagination" and remarked that "it is when Miró is at his boldest that he turns out his most compelling pictures." The relative ill-success of this exhibition did not deflect the artist from his chosen path. Two months later, at Montroig, he began *The Farm*, continued working on it at Barcelona and, taking "two sample tufts of grass" with him to Paris, completed it there, after eight months' work all told.

In Paris Miró found a climate propitious to the flowering of his art, though at first his shyness and retiring disposition made it hard for him to feel at ease in his new surroundings. For this was the time when confusion reigned in the Parisian art world, and nothing could have been more foreign to his temperament than the belligerence and noisy self-assertion of the "angry young men" of Montparnasse in the post-war years. But a sure instinct led him to associate with artists of his own caliber and to center his attention on works of real value though still little known (for example those of Paul Klee from 1924 onward and of Kandinsky), many of which fell in line with his own aspirations.

The curious glamour of that period and its mood of feverish excitement have been described by many of those who played a part in it. Robert Desnos, speaking of Miró's studio, mentions "that courtyard, a typically Parisian phenomenon," which consisted of a grassy plot with a lilac tree and a vine, "where birds made music in summer and where, in winter, the snow was whiter and stayed longer than elsewhere in Paris." "It was about this time," Jacques Viot wrote (*Cahiers d'Art*, 1-4, 1934), "that I used to go to see him in that dilapidated house at the end of a row of courtyards strewn with litter, where Miró, reacting against the squalor of the age, whitewashed his studio and disinfected it, carefully numbered his brushes, installed a régime of scrupulous tidiness, played havoc with all he had been taught and, protected by a habit of extreme politeness and also by the then general incomprehension of what he had in mind, declared his intention of 'wringing the neck of painting'— and promptly set to work!" Georges Limbour tells us that "never within the group (if group it can be called) which was working out its own enlightenment, without a thought for publicity or the outside world, were there any rivalries, quarrels, intrigues, dissemblings or attempts to outdo each other. A wonderful fraternity and mutual trust reigned among these young, dedicated artists" (Preface to *Conversations between Georges Charbonnier and André Masson*, Paris, 1958).

1923 was the crucial year. That summer, at Montroig, Miró's art underwent a decisive change: a change, however, that was the logical result of all that had gone before and in which he kept to, but enlarged on, familiar material. Three pictures on Catalan themes—*The Tilled Field* (Clifford Collection, Radnor, U.S.A.), *Pastoral* (Duchamp Collection, New York) and *The Hunter* (Museum of Modern Art)—mark the successive steps. In *The Tilled Field* we have all the elements previously employed: farm, trees, pine and cactus; the animals still are isolated and all are treated on the same scale—rooster, snail, rabbits, dog, oxen, fish—but some have developed strange excrescences. Fur and feathers bristle with spines; the pine tree has a huge ear and an eye. In *Pastoral* the composition is less dense and the realistic details from which the picture started are gradually attenuated, until all that remains is a skeleton design, like a draftsman's plan. In *The Hunter* this spareness is carried a stage further; non-functional elements are indicated by a thread, a line or quite simple geometric forms. The peasant's head, eye, mustache, ear and pipe are fitted into a triangle with a cap above it (the red Catalan cap, vaguely Phrygian in aspect, known as a *barretina*), all being joined by a connecting thread to the man's ultra-schematized limbs. With one hand he holds the animal he has shot, a rabbit (hinted at by a few suggestive lines) and with the other the black, cylindrical mass of his gun. Some dotted lines, symbolizing life, wind round the central structure of the body. Only essential organs—heart and genitals—are clearly indicated. True, each of the smaller figures, tiny air-borne automata, can be "interpreted," but what above all charms the eye is the all-pervasive rhythm, like that of an aerial ballet planned by a fancy-free choreographer.

The hard thinking that lay behind the making of these pictures is perhaps even more apparent in the works produced by Miró on his return to Paris in early 1924. Some were left on the canvas almost in the state of drawings, notably the *Spanish Dancer* and *Portrait of Madame K.* in the René Gaffé Collection. Turning his back on the lures of color and drawing in charcoal on a pale grey ground executed in tempera, Miró applied himself to depicting with rigorous precision the "working parts" of the human body. He also had recourse to concrete geometric elements, such as the draftsman's triangle and the flat rulers, which act as the support to the composition (the body as a whole is set within a rhombus, either drawn in or implied); also to signs having for him a magical significance: a flaming heart, the black mass of a head with Gorgonesque hair, breasts placed at the ends of an axial line, one represented frontally and the other in side-view.

THE HARLEQUIN'S CARNIVAL, 1924-1925.
ALBRIGHT-KNOX ART GALLERY, BUFFALO, N.Y.

In *Maternity* (Penrose Collection), painted entirely in oils, we have the end-product of these remarkable experiments. It has an engaging simplicity, not a trace is left of hesitation or overloading and all the preliminary linework is omitted. Upon a field whose translucency is suggested here and there by glints of blue and yellow, the figure of the mother is solidly mounted on a convex triangle, at once a sexual symbol and an indication of the body's mass; like a toy figure which, though flexible, cannot be turned because it rests on a leaden base, the woman's figure seems to sway, her head thrown back. A second axial line cuts through the median line in the center of the canvas and at its extremities are the breasts from which dangle a female child with a milk-white sphere (the moon) and a male child with a black sun inset. There is a truly cosmic quality in this work, despite the quite amazing economy of means employed and the piquant wit of its conception.

The Harlequin's Carnival (Buffalo) ranks as the climactic work of this period. Painted in the winter of 1924-1925, at the artist's studio in Rue Blomet, it might be described as an "interior" version of The Tilled Field and in it Miró returns to his detailed, meticulous execution, keeping well in hand the tumultuous inward drive to which he was now by way of giving expression. Extremely complex but never overloaded, the composition is built up quite straightforwardly around the central figure, a man playing a guitar. The wire-drawn axis of his body, duplicated by a white spiral, bisects the canvas vertically, and is divided horizontally by the line formed by the junction of the floor and wall, and also by an arm ending in a monstrous hand. This intersection, though twice repeated, is not pronounced enough to disturb the overall balance, but acts on the contrary as a unifying factor. The second structural element is the ladder on the left, reaching to the extreme foreground, and towards which converge a series of diagonals that, too, are never overemphasized. On the picture surface thus divided up schematically we see a host of small, wonderfully lively figures, no longer isolated (as in early works) but linked together—cats playing with skeins of wool, frolicking butterflies, tiny flying manikins with extended arms, joining in the carnival. Their movements are curiously mechanical; a butterfly darts out of

PAINTING, 1925. MADAME MARIE CUTTOLI COLLECTION, PARIS.

a container like a jack-in-the-box and the central figure is held up by a spring. Colors play an important part in the legibility and balance of the forms. They tell out upon the faintly mottled ground of floor and wall with an insistence that stresses volumes and plastic values. Moreover they are arranged in such a way that none overrides the others, the only accent being supplied by passages of the blue for which Miró has always had a penchant and which figures on certain more or less extended planes at selected points—the table, the patch of sky in the window, the comet's tail, the butterflies' wings—and which strikes as it were a deeper note providing zones of rest in the general agitation. But where is Harlequin? it may be asked. He is in the left-hand sector, half way up, and forms the only (relatively) static element in the riot of movement he is contemplating with a placid eye. Despite his comical outfit, his clownish cap, his up-twirled mustache and long smoke-plumed pipe, he looks sad. He represents the typical Catalan peasant or perhaps, with his big round head, Miró himself, watcher and donor of this strange masterwork of a modern Primitive.

We can well understand that Miró's adhesion, following Masson's, to the Surrealist movement was regarded as a note-worthy event. For he had already achieved in his art "that fusion of two states, seeming so incompatible—reality and the dream— in a sort of absolute reality, a super-reality" which Breton hoped for. Looking back on this in his *Genèse et perspective artistiques du surréalisme* (1941), Breton wrote: "The sensational entrance of Miró in 1924 marked an important date in the development of surrealist art. Miró, who already had to his credit an œuvre which, if less advanced in spirit, had plastic qualities of the highest order, crossed at one leap the final barriers restraining him from total spontaneity of expression. From now on his work displays an innocence and a freedom that has never been surpassed. There are reasons for believing that his influence was largely the determining factor when Picasso joined forces with Surrealism two years later." This last phrase shows that the opinions of the young, little known painter already carried weight among his brother-artists.

Surrealism, reciprocally, helped to draw attention to Miró's art. When Jacques Viot organized his second one-man show (June 12 to June 27, 1925) at the Galerie Pierre, all the Surrealists signed the invitation to the exhibition and Benjamin Péret contributed a preface. Thirty-one paintings, among them *The Farm* (subsequently bought by Ernest Hemingway), and fifteen drawings were exhibited. The opening day was the occasion of a surrealist demonstration which attracted a large crowd. Five months later Miró took part in an exhibition of Surrealist Painting held under the auspices of Breton and Desnos in the same gallery, one of the three recent pictures he sent in being *The Harlequin's Carnival*. There were also works by Klee and Picasso.

The Surrealists advocated an entirely new approach to the creative process, involving a collective use of "psychic automatism and a systematic derangement of the senses," with a view to opening up a field of pure imagination, and enlarging the domain of all the creative arts. For a certain time, in association with the Surrealists, if slightly aloof from them, the group of young men who forgathered in the Rue Blomet had been experimenting on these lines. Miró, however, was not to be deflected from his path and kept to his fixed hours of work, his personal disciplines. None the less he was gradually infected with the nervous tension of his friends, all the more so since his powers of resistance were weakened by the lack of regular meals and the feverish unrest induced by constant brooding on the problems of his art. A time came when, under certain conditions, he began to "dream" his paintings and to impart to his world of forms, hitherto so strongly rooted in reality, a willfully

PAINTING, 1924. PRIVATE COLLECTION.

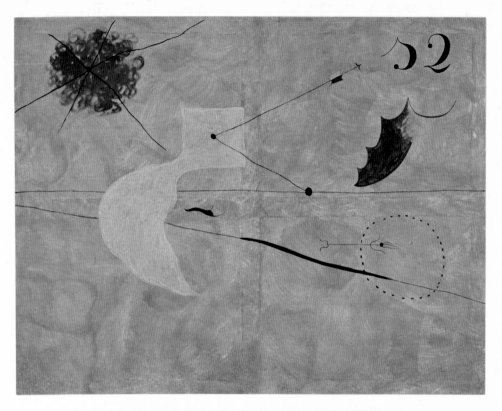

THE SIESTA, 1925. MADAME MARIE CUTTOLI COLLECTION, PARIS.

dreamlike aspect. This phase lasted three years (1925-1927) and
gave rise to a considerable body of work of this description,
to which, however, Miró did not confine himself exclusively.
It largely depended on the conditions under which he worked;
thus when he made his yearly stay at Montroig, he regained his

foothold in reality and his manner changed. This did not prevent his transposing elements from one domain into the other, just as he always based even his wildest fantasies on fragments of concrete experience.

There are about a hundred of these "dream pictures" and the surprisingly large number can be explained as being a spontaneous demonstration of his hard-won freedom. For on the face of it they are at the opposite pole from Miró's insistence on details, or perhaps it would be more accurate to suggest that, after experiencing such a multitude of impulses, he felt that each was worthy of being developed separately and given independent plastic expression. These somewhat enigmatic works (many have remained in the possession of persons with whom he was friendly at the time, and they were rarely exhibited) have so extreme a spareness, and are so deficient in any anecdotal elements giving a clue to their interpretation that, except to an understanding eye, they may well seem almost pointless. Yet they are of much interest not only for their intrinsic excellence but also for the light they throw on Miró's prescience of certain new directives that have only recently come to the fore. The Musée d'Art Moderne of Paris was well advised in giving them a prominent place in the retrospective exhibition of 1962.

Of all the artist's works these are the most "surrealist" in spirit; they often seem to have been made in a state of hypnosis or with the eyes shut, the artist's hand, once it begins to move, following its own bent, tensing or relaxing automatically, guided by unconscious reflexes. In the same way as the poet for whom the rhyme precedes the idea, suggests and imposes it, Miró now for the first time relies on the physical properties of the medium *per se*, its capacity for working out its own solutions. This procedure was to stand him in good stead when he took to making ceramics. In a radio talk with Georges Charbonnier in 1960 he said: "Never, never do I set to work on a canvas in the state it comes in from the shop. I provoke accidents—a form, a splotch of color. Any accident is good enough. I let the *matière* decide. Then I prepare a ground by, for example, wiping my brushes on the canvas. Letting fall some drops of turpentine on

BONHEUR D'AIMER MA BRUNE, 1925.
COLLECTION OF M. AND MME RAYMOND QUENEAU, NEUILLY-SUR-SEINE.

it would do just as well. If I want to make a drawing I crumple the sheet of paper or I wet it; the flowing water traces a line and this line may suggest what is to come next... The painter works like the poet; first the word, then the thought. I attach much importance to the initial shock."

PAINTING, 1925. TRISTAN TZARA COLLECTION, PARIS.

THE CIRCUS, 1925. COLLECTION OF MR AND MRS RALPH F. COLIN, NEW YORK.

These remarks (which sum up the program of not a few of the young painters of today) describe a method which is already thirty-five years old. But what may seem surprising is that Miró changed over so abruptly to a viewpoint apparently so incompatible with all his previous, carefully planned works. We must remember that among the young men he associated with in 1925 there were more writers than painters (hence he was less on his guard against them) and that thanks to this association he shared in a number of exciting and rewarding experiences. So far he had always pursued a solitary path, and these contacts not only widened his horizons but had effects that were not merely on the surface. Though he never took sides in any of the personal feuds of the group or joined in their political activities, he was basically in sympathy with Breton and his friends as regards the new techniques they advocated and their objectives. He always joined in all the group exhibitions and, even when cold-shouldered or attacked by his friends, remained loyal to them. There is no question that Miró found in Surrealism a real source of inspiration and in transposing its "message" into his own domain of art—needless to say, on his own lines—did more than any other, in the years 1925-1927, to make good in practice the surrealist theories of painting.

In this new phase color played a predominant role. It now became autonomous, all-pervasive, independent of all it used to illustrate. Most, however, of the "dream pictures" are monochrome, their vast expanses somewhat blurred and indefinite, animated only by drifting, cloudlike undulations in which occasionally a tracery of dotted lines seems to revive a motif or memory of the past. Here and there solid bodies or streaks of white having the forms and substance of living beings emerge, whose meaning gradually reveals itself. Sometimes, too, in this undefined space, sky or netherworld, we glimpse the sudden transit of a meteor, a comet's trail, a falling rocket.

The series of paintings of this type titled *The Circus Horse* might be described as an intellectual exercise—or extravaganza. First, the form of the horse and the rider's whip are hinted at by an elongated white patch on a dark ground, its sharp, expressive contours traced by meanders of the whiplash. Next, the entire theme is enveloped by a single arabesque and forms

PAINTING, 1927. TRISTAN TZARA COLLECTION, PARIS.

LASSO, 1927. GEORGES DUTHUIT COLLECTION, PARIS.

are still suggested by an interplay of downstrokes and upstrokes. In a final version the theme fades out completely; all we see is a simple, sinuous line inscribed on empty space, which, like a magic lasso, traps our gaze.

In some pictures of this phase Miró makes use of letters, key-words or poetic phrases serving both as explanatory comments and as compositional factors. Other forms are so sharply demarcated as to produce the effect of a *trompe-l'œil* arrangement of pasted paper, anticipating Miró's ingenious use of *papiers collés* (much closer to Dadaism and Arp than to Cubism) in 1928-1929. Perhaps his move from Rue Blomet to a studio in Montmartre (Rue Tourlaque), where he had for neighbors Max Ernst, Magritte, Eluard and Arp, had something to do with this new departure. He became particularly intimate with Eluard, a book of whose poems he subsequently illustrated, and also with Arp, who has valiantly denied that (as some have said) he in any way influenced his friend.

Thus this part of Miró's œuvre cannot be disassociated from Surrealism, and doubtless this applies also to the compositions, few in number and unusually elaborate, of the summers of 1926 and 1927 (exhibited at the Bernheim Gallery in 1928 under the aegis of Pierre Loeb). These works have landscape settings, clearly indicated as such, though the colors are far removed from those of nature, and the figures, while deriving from Catalan folk art (already used by Miró), undergo fantastic avatars, grotesque enlargements of certain features, minglings of different species and reversions to embryonic forms. Acquired by museums overseas, these well-known works have tended to divert attention from their contemporaries produced in Paris. True, they are more accomplished, more schematic and thus more striking than the latter, but they were conceived in a different spirit. The *Person Throwing a Stone at a Bird* (Museum of Modern Art) is based on the contrast between the figure (an enormous foot, a body shaped like the calf of a leg, attached directly to a small round head) and the graceful wisp-like bird with a fiery crest. In the *Dog Barking at the Moon* (Philadelphia), it is largely the undulation of the line between the brown earth and the night sky that creates the eerie atmosphere in which a strange animal with a semi-human head is baying its helpless passion for a no less peculiar orb, vaguely reminiscent of a topsy-turvy bird. Yet a way of access lies open, a Jacob's ladder on the left leading to some high realm of the super-conscious. At this stage Miró's transfigurations of things and beings have reached a point where "literal" meanings cease to count; they have become signs that the artist, following some secret train of thought, has conjured up out of the recesses of his mind. Yet, even though we cannot decipher them, their very strangeness has a curiously compelling power and these pregnant images haunt the mind long after we cease looking at them.

Miró was now to embark on two interesting ventures in which he utilized the technical means he had recently tested out, first with a view to enlarging the picture content, then as a means of stripping it down to bare essentials. During a fortnight's stay in Holland in 1928, he had been greatly struck by the interior scenes of the Dutch seventeenth-century painters and he now decided to reinterpret in his manner the themes of certain picture postcards which he took home to Paris. Hence the three large canvases known as Miró's "Dutch Interiors." The first (Museum of Modern Art) derived from H.M. Sorgh's *Lute Player* (Rijksmuseum, Amsterdam), the second (Peggy Guggenheim Collection, Venice) from Jan Steen's *The Cat's Dancing Lesson* (Rijksmuseum) and the third (Marx Collection, New York) from a mythological scene. He followed these up, in 1929, with the four "Imaginary Portraits," based on reproductions of works in museums. Miró has kept the preliminary sketches for both these sequences, and they show the successive stages by which he arrived at the final picture. In his excellent study of *Dutch Interior II*, Jacques Dupin has published Jan Steen's picture, the drawings showing Miró's tentative alterations of certain details, and his first version of the entire composition. Dupin also reproduces the series of preliminary sketches, beginning with a schematic diagram, made by Miró for the

DOG BARKING AT THE MOON, 1926.
A.E. GALLATIN COLLECTION, PHILADELPHIA MUSEUM OF ART.

DUTCH INTERIOR I, 1928. COLLECTION, THE MUSEUM OF MODERN ART, NEW YORK. MRS SIMON GUGGENHEIM FUND.

DUTCH INTERIOR II, 1928. PEGGY GUGGENHEIM COLLECTION, VENICE.

Portrait of Queen Louise of Prussia. Mr James Sweeney has eluci-
dated the origins of the *Portrait of a Lady of 1820*, after Constable
(Art News Annual, 1954), and Mr J. T. Soby has traced the origin
of the *Portrait of Mrs Mills in 1750* to a portrait by George
Engelheart, a pupil of Reynolds. Last of the "Imaginary Portraits" is the one of "La Fornarina," after Raphael.

That the "Dutch Interiors" are in the direct lineage of *The
Harlequin's Carnival* is particularly evident in the first of the series.
Here the composition is exceptionally detailed, crowded with
small figures, quaintly shaped animals and such oddities as the
starfish-like hand on the guitar and the vertical footprints. Here
we have another illustration of Miró's habit of following up
certain procedures over a considerable period, even when
introducing new ones as well. In fact he never hesitates to
utilize discoveries made in other circumstances and, paradoxically
enough, this helps to speed up his evolution.

As regards the "Dutch Interiors," it seems to me of less
interest trying to identify, behind the deformations (of the same
kind as in the preceding works), the prototypal images used by
Miró as his points of departure, than to note the way in which
he imposes a "tight, cohesive planning" on seemingly incompatible ingredients. This aspect of the problem may very well have
attracted him as being a challenge to his ingenuity. But of more
interest in our opinion is an attempt to ascertain the idea behind
the metamorphosis, which involved a regrouping of the foreign
elements and giving them a wholly new significance.

To begin with, we would draw attention to the way in
which, in *Interior II*, needless details of the Steen picture—the
pitcher, the chair, the window, the viol (changed into a guitar)—
have been either suppressed or reduced to microscopic dimensions, the effect being greatly to increase the available picture
space. The figures, on the other hand, have been prodigiously
enlarged, the one on the left becoming merely a gigantic head,

fully recognizable, however, when we turn to the laughing face in the Steen "original." But Miró is not content with reproducing in a general way and with much dexterity, the arrangement of the picture elements in his model; he aims above all at emphasizing the links between them and the movement bringing them

PORTRAIT OF QUEEN LOUISE OF PRUSSIA, 1929.
PIERRE MATISSE GALLERY, NEW YORK.

LA FORNARINA (AFTER RAPHAEL), 1929. GALERIE MAEGHT, PARIS.

to life. This is why he makes two parts of an enormous serpent emerge from the dog's body and, enclosing the whole composition, give it a rhythm answering to the position of each figure and stressing the part it plays in the ensemble. In these two series of pictures the geometric division of the picture space, which existed in the preliminary sketch and plays a dominant role in *The Harlequin's Carnival,* is replaced by swirling rhythms set up by massive spirals, which also modify the contours of figures and objects. In *Interior I* this rhythm, instead of surrounding the picture elements, inheres in the sinuous body of the central figure—the lute-player transformed into a guitarist— and in the savage twist given his face, and it impregnates everything around him.

In the "Imaginary Portraits" Miró returns to the problem at the point where he had dropped it and reaches a seemingly definitive solution. The ostensible subject counts for him less and less. Often Miró himself has forgotten the names of the pictures which acted as his taking-off points. In *Queen Louise of Prussia* a wholly different idea, inspired by a reproduction of a Diesel motor, grafted itself on to the original theme. In the portraits there is no longer any attempt to "entertain" the spectator, the only exception being the first of the series, *Portrait of Mrs Mills in 1750,* where some graphic details still remain. Elsewhere the whole structure is based on an interplay of colored masses, given a glossy finish or roughened, according to differences of planes. In the *Lady of 1820* the curiously protoplasmic body seems to swell or contract at will. In *Queen Louise* all that remains of the figure is a hollow arabesque, a bell-shaped formation gliding towards a corner of the picture, while the picture as a whole suggests a stage with, on the left, a broad black upright, like a strip of scenery. Last of the series is *La Fornarina,* a shadowy form hardly distinguishable from the shadows whence it emerges, the only distinct element being the minute black head, in front of which a daintily drawn white fish suggests the flash of a sidelong glance from the tiny eye centering a nimbus-like pool of shadows. There is nothing in this strangely insubstantial figure on which the gaze can fix; drawing, color, even subject count for little, and we are conscious only of a "presence," elusive, unforgettable.

This first phase of Miró's œuvre (spanning some ten or eleven years) was marked by a series of outstanding successes. Step by step he assembled all the elements of a highly personal art, mastering stage by stage the disciplines of drawing, color and composition. In so doing he proceeded from the most complex to the simplest forms (giving his interpretations a singular clarity and inevitability), and from strictly geometric arrangements to a pictorial architecture that was always implicit, never on the surface. He disassembled the "working parts" of living beings and things and, by depicting them with complete autonomy of means and rearranging them in a new order, invested them with a significance at once general and particular, and an evocative power like that of archetypal myths and esoteric figurations. Though no one had a clearer insight into the secrets of the natural world, Miró never became a slave to them, but used them as a means both to the exploration of the human psyche and to the expression of a cosmic imagery. And in so doing he clothed the imaginary with convincing form. Indeed his entire output of this period, at once copious and eclectic, bears the stamp of a personality unique of its kind.

THE PAINTER'S DILEMMA
RESEARCH AND READJUSTMENT

Soleil de proie, prisonnier de ma tête
Enlève la colline, enlève la forêt...

PAUL ELUARD

SUCH a series of unqualified successes, even if it found so far no recognition on the material plane, ranked Miró from the very start among the foremost artists of the day. But, as was to be expected, it involved some setbacks. Whenever his perspicacity or tenacity of purpose led him to the logical consequences of a new approach, the rankling unrest forever inherent in his temperament led him to envisage new solutions and to doubt the validity of his discoveries. And now he felt a need for calling everything in question, for re-appraising and, if needs be, repudiating all that he had so far pinned his faith to, in order to secure a solid, well-tried starting point for a new departure—though even this, he knew, would still lack the comforting assurance of being definitive. For a craving for "total purity" is fundamental to Miró's attitude to art.

The testing time came in 1929, with the beginning of a series of upheavals in the outside world from which Miró suffered all the more keenly because he refused to externalize his feelings. This phase, which lasted for a little over a decade, was one of the most trying experiences of his career. It was as if he had to force his way along an uphill path, strewn with obstacles and

PAPIER COLLÉ, SUMMER 1929. PRIVATE COLLECTION, PARIS.

perilous abysses, and the ordeal came to an end—at the cost of painful struggles—only when the artist realized that the world to which he truly belonged lay elsewhere.

The notion of "wringing the neck of painting" (an expression that Miró, echoing Marcel Duchamp, was fond of using at this time) had been given currency some years before in the heyday of Dada. But the Surrealists were already tackling the problem from another angle. Even when given a wider context than that of a technique—sometimes exaggerated *ad absurdum*—their program involved a revision of all traditional standards of art, a glorification of non-conformity as such, and a search for new, effective means suggested by this refusal to toe the line.

Miró toyed with this revolutionary notion for some time before committing himself to it, but in the result he took it more seriously than most of its exponents and once again his intransigence and singleness of purpose led him to extreme measures. Some of the sacrifices this entailed must have gone against the grain, since he had reason to believe that he had already solved his problems and come to terms with the urge to painterly perfection that had become a second nature with him. None the less, once he had committed himself, he did not hesitate to discard or disregard—if only momentarily—the extraordinary sleight of hand he had acquired. So now he struck out in a new direction with a dogged, sometimes almost desperate resolve.

During the winter of 1928-1929, in his experimental sketches, Miró began to hold in check the spontaneity of his drawing and his penchant for the arabesque by breaking up the line so savagely as to produce effects of brutal abruptness, even clumsiness. In a first series of *collages-objets* he substituted for the "interpretation" of a subject, a simple juxtaposition of neutral, characterless oddments: nails, bits of string, torn or crumpled strips of sandpaper and linoleum. Yet even with these uncompromising materials he brought off miracles of grace such as the

Spanish Dancer so aptly described by Paul Eluard as "a picture of an unimaginable nudity: just a hat-pin and a wing-feather on the virgin canvas."

In the summer of 1929 Miró reverted to this procedure and employed it in a series of large *papiers collés* which were exhibited at the Galerie Pierre in 1930. They were given a place of honor alongside cubist works by Picasso and Braque and collages by Ernst, Duchamp and Arp in the "Collages" exhibition at the Galerie Goemans, introduced by Aragon's aggressively titled text: *Challenge to Painting*. The structure of these pictures was such that the materials employed, exceptional as they were, seemed perfectly appropriate. Miró adjusted his line to the forms suggested by the shapes of the torn fragments and the reliefs produced by recourse to a collage deliberately left irregular and unfinished. The drawing becomes bolder when the material used is of superior quality and invites broader rhythms, but everywhere the line is prepotent and clearly defines forms.

The superb craftsmanship of this group of works points the way to the large compositions of 1933, based on preliminary collages, and also to the *dessins-collages* of the same period. Here Miró disposes, with unfailing elegance, wholly incongruous anecdotal elements: sentimental postcards, butterflies, figures or images clipped out of advertisements placed at the tips of elongated branch-like structures suggestive of human figures. But his figurations are so personal and he handles his far-ranging arabesques with such originality that they carry complete conviction. Moreover, he has a gift for integrating all sorts of "foreign bodies" ready to hand that serve his turn.

Here we may note that Miró's art is at its intensest when he employs a soft instrument such as a graphite pencil. The bold experiments he made in the summer of 1931 at Montroig, of painting with pigment diluted with turpentine on "Ingres" paper, proved, in my opinion, to be a failure. His practice here

PAPIER COLLÉ, SUMMER 1929.
P. BRUGUIÈRE COLLECTION, ISSY-LES-MOULINEAUX (SEINE).

was to apply directly pure, more or less diluted colors to the white ground, these colors being placed in simple horizontal, vertical or diagonal bands, independently of any form, and giving an impression that the painter's concern at this stage was solely to "animate" the surface, as the fancy took him. Having thus prepared his ground, Miró added human figures, reduced to elementary, almost abstract signs and circumscribed with uniform black contours. The best of these somewhat brashly executed works are in the Urvater Collection (Brussels) and that of Madame Cuttoli. Only incidentally do we find elements of Miró's previous repertory; they remind us, rather, of Picasso's sculptures in wire. By and large they do not seem to have interesting possibilities, except perhaps in the field of decoration.

A final exhibition of *collages-objets*, entitled "Sculptures," took place in December 1931 at the Galerie Pierre. The artist's daring conjunctions of the most unlikely and incongruous elements caught the eye of Massine, who promptly commissioned Miró to design the sets and costumes of his new ballet, *Jeux d'Enfants*. Miró started work at once and, using elementary signs inspired by his most recent ventures, made the curtain, scenery and costumes for this ballet, which had a good reception at Monte Carlo on April 14, 1932. Only a few sketches have survived. The team-work involved in the making of a ballet appealed to Miró and he often expressed his regret that another opportunity of the kind never came his way.

Meanwhile his art had been enriched by discoveries made in this experimental period, which had lasted for three years, and when he now reverted to his familiar vocabulary, the main stream of his painting, he brought to it wider knowledge and new technical resources. In summer 1932 he worked in the quietude of Montroig, and in the following months at Barcelona. For some years a change had been coming over his way of life. After his marriage to Pilar Juncosa, who came of a Mallorcan family, in 1929 and the birth of his daughter Dolores at Barcelona in 1931, he took to making longer stays in Catalonia. Meanwhile he had given up his studio in Paris and rented a small three-room apartment in the southern district of the city. Here he was cut off to some extent from his surrealist friends (who in any case were now becoming much obsessed with politics) and working conditions were less satisfactory. Moreover at this time the art world of Paris was being hard hit by the world-wide slump, and avant-garde galleries were liable to close their doors at short notice. Under these conditions Miró found the atmosphere at Montroig and even of Barcelona (where he had refitted his studio) more favorable to steady work.

The group of twelve small paintings on wooden panels made in 1932 may be described as a résumé of the possible variations of a woman's body subjected to organic distortions. With an objective, meticulously observant eye, the painter watches the resultant mutations in the inner life of forms. The physical aspect of the figures suggests potential acts and gestures, and the distortions are a logical corollary of these diverse possibilities. Despite the small size of these panels, bodies achieve a monumental solidity, and the plangent, full-bodied colors meet in accords of an astringency that rasps the eye. These panels were exhibited in a small gallery recently opened by Pierre Colle in Rue Cambacérès, and form a link between Miró's earlier and his new phase.

This begins with the eighteen big paintings made from March to June 1933 in his Barcelona studio. All derived from collages, the reason being that Miró was determined to exclude any lingering effect of memory and of the training his hand had undergone—i.e. of all acquired habits—and to create totally concrete forms. In order to arrive at this supreme detachment and discipline of his creative powers, he devised a curious procedure. For each picture he built up a preliminary collage

COMPOSITION, 1933.
COLLECTION OF MR AND MRS KLAUS G. PERLS, NEW YORK.

70

by disposing on plain white cardboard small photographs cut out of newspapers or catalogues, representing household utensils, machines and the like, none of them having any aesthetic value or significance. Next, he tacked these groups of "neutral" objects on to the wall of his studio and fell to painting them as if he had before his eyes a living model. Using these trivial, inert elements as points of departure, he succeeded in creating truly elemental, finely balanced figures.

This group of pictures represents one of the peak points of his œuvre; they are charged with a concentrated power, a plastic dynamism, that, surely, has never been surpassed. Without the least recourse to any anecdotal allusion that might distract our attention, the signs and figures they contain achieve a breath-taking expressiveness and fully justify the unusual procedure that went to their making. Miró has kept the preliminary collages (they have never been exhibited, being mere pointers) and when we compare them with the pictures, the exact source of every pictorial element can be traced, though there is no obvious relationship between them. In the picture the most insignificant object becomes an hieratic sign or figure of a very real grandeur; where, on the collage, there was a seeming-casual juxtaposition of irrelevant items, the development of the forms has brought about an organic coherence, and instilled into them a new meaning. Seemingly Miró did not reach this point by gradual degrees (as with his "Dutch Interiors") but by a swift and sudden act of the will, transmuting, in a single operation, base metal into gold.

In these works no form is positively recognizable, limited that is to say to only one interpretation; but, on the other hand, none is gratuitous, since behind it lies a fragment of reality, and each is the nucleus of a mass of suggestions. Structured in black and white enhanced with accents of pure color, these forms develop freely on subtly modulated backgrounds bathed in a soft inner radiance and creating an atmosphere of mystery. These basic elements of a new language, drawn together by a sort of capillary attraction into groupings having a distinctive rhythm, are charged with significance, apart from any question of their individual meanings. Miró has always denied being an abstractionist. "How can it be said," he asked Georges Duthuit (*Cahiers d'Art*, 1936, No. 8-10), "that, given the fact that all the signs I transcribe upon the canvas correspond to something concrete—how can it be said that they lack a foundation in reality, do not form part of the real world?" The type of formal perfection he had now arrived at makes itself felt once more in a group of large paintings intended to serve as cartoons for tapestries. Commissioned by Madame Cuttoli, they were made in 1937 and, not being forced to conform to a preliminary collage, they are more freely executed. Out of a colorful maze of mobile forms, figures arise spontaneously and interlock in arrangements which are sometimes implemented by written words figuring on the canvas: for example, *Hirondelle Amour*, *Escargot Femme Fleur Etoile*.

Thus from a series of experiments which at first sight seemed negative, incoherent and all but incomprehensible, Miró derived the sources of what is perhaps the most "classical" manifestation of his genius, and a means to the creation of a purely plastic language. However, when these admirable works were shown in 1933 at the Bernheim Gallery (the exhibition was organized by Pierre Loeb), they did not have the success they merited. As a result of the depression, Loeb had to give up his activities as Miró's dealer, but he continued to speak highly of his work; in 1945 he still had some of these pictures in his possession and regaled his friends with them.

This seems the place for a tribute to the understanding few who championed Miró's art from the start. After Dalmau and Maurice Raynal, Loeb organized all Miró's exhibitions in Paris

PAINTING (TAPESTRY CARTOON), 1934.
PHILIPPE DOTREMONT COLLECTION, BRUSSELS.

COLLAGE PAINTING ON SANDPAPER, 1934.
A.E. GALLATIN COLLECTION, PHILADELPHIA MUSEUM OF ART.

from 1925 to 1933, and Pierre Matisse followed suit in New York. Since then no less than fifteen "anthological," well-balanced exhibitions (accompanied by invaluable catalogues), covering every aspect of Miró's œuvre, have been organized by Pierre Matisse. In 1928 Jeanne Bucher commissioned Miró's first illustrated book. René Gaffé was the first collector to purchase several of Miró's pictures and some of his Belgian friends followed suit. Madame Cuttoli acquired several of the most abstruse compositions before commissioning in 1934 the remarkable, relatively straightforward tapestry cartoons described above. Lastly, from 1931 on, Christian Zervos in *Cahiers d'Art*, and from 1933 on Albert Skira in *Minotaure* gave Miró a place of honor in these periodicals. Of particular interest is No. 1-4 (1934) of *Cahiers d'Art* which begins with a "homage to Miró" of no less than fifty-eight pages, comprising *inter alia* the first systematic study of his œuvre (up to 1933) by Zervos, the prefaces by Raynal and Benjamin Péret to the catalogues of his first exhibitions in Paris, texts by Gaffé, Grohmann, Hemingway, Huidobro, Herbert Read, J. J. Sweeney, and "souvenirs" by Robert Desnos and Jacques Viot. This special number contains reproductions of outstanding works and his most recent experimental compositions, and includes two color plates, ample documentation and bibliographical data. From the *Cahiers* we learn that the first art museums to acquire works by Miró were those at Grenoble, Stockholm (thanks to Ragnar Hoppe), Hartford and, at New York, what was then the Museum of Living Art (Gallatin Collection). A year later *Minotaure* No. 7 had a cover, in full color, by Miró.

This consecration of his art by the leading connoisseurs of the day (whose interest in his work even at its most "outrageous" never flagged), the unclouded happiness of his family life and his inspired solutions of the perplexities of his early phase seemed to assure for Miró, then at the height of his powers, a brilliantly successful future. But now his peace of mind was shattered and his hitherto carefree art abruptly plunged into an atmosphere of gloom charged with the tragic sense of life. This was due, not to any personal misfortune, but to the darkening of the political horizon and the unleashing of blind, insensate passions. Two dates mark successive stages of the cataclysmic break-up of the western world: 1936, the beginning of the civil war in Spain, and 1939 that of the World War; and on top of these there were the racial persecutions and the Moscow trials. As early as 1934 we find symptoms in Miró's art of a haunting premonition of disaster. It was in the summer of that year that he began the series of pastels on velvet-surface paper that may be regarded as the prelude to what he himself called his *peintures sauvages*.

Grotesque effigies, often imbued with a morbidly erotic suggestiveness, make their appearance, and human bodies undergo Circean transformations. Feet become paws, limbs assume the shape of insects' wingcases or dwindle to stumps, while mouths turn into razor-edged beaks, teeth into fangs. Unsightly growths of hair sprout on crania and armpits. Yet the backgrounds of these monstrous forms are executed with an extreme delicacy, all in tender hues, elusive nuances, and the general effect produced is one of caricatures or "the imaginings of a gifted child." But in the paintings made in winter 1935 and those of the following spring—usually on hard supports, masonite or copper—they become actively alarming. In these strange works ferocity runs riot, deformations are stressed by brutal elongations and splashes of color stepped up to its maximum intensity: sulfurous yellows, fiery reds. Volumes are corroded by curious fungoid growths. Despite their small dimensions, these paintings are replete with eerie figures dispersed in landscapes strewn with volcanos and barren wastelands under a lurid sky. The very titles are revealing: *Men and Women facing a Heap of Excrement, Persons in the Presence of a Metamorphosis, Persons attracted by the Form of a Mountain.* In these pictures we watch the portentous birth-pangs of figures whose hybrid forms seem to be molded by the upheavals of their natural environment.

All these works were produced first at Montroig, then in Barcelona, during the months of ever-rising tension which preceded the outbreak of civil war in July 1936. Then, returning to Montroig, Miró set to work on a sequence of twenty-seven pictures on masonite panels all of exactly the same size. These comprise a series of variations on certain elementary forms that seem to have obsessed the artist during this period. Close-knit, based on contrasts of black and white, they are executed in the most banal materials: ripolin enamel, coal-tar casein and sand. To my mind we have here not so much a protest, a gesture of revolt, as a resolute, almost tranquil assertion of the stability of Miró's private world confronted by the rising storm. The distortions have no longer the monstrousness of those of the previous phase; it is as though the event itself were less alarming than its expectation.

In the autumn Miró returned to Paris. Having now no apartment or studio, he stayed for the time being in a humble Montparnasse hotel (Rue Jules Chaplain), and joined forces with the students at the Grande-Chaumière where like them he drew from the figure. The dozens of drawings of nudes he made there were brutal to an extreme; under grossly swollen muscles and ravaged skin all semblance of humanity is lost, faces are reduced to ugly excrescences, nothing is spared by the ruthless line. But Miró's imagination was, it seemed, running dry; he could hardly bring himself to paint. Working on the floor of the Galerie Pierre, he took five months to complete a single canvas, the *Still Life with Old Shoe* (J. T. Soby Collection, New Canaan, Conn.). The humble subject—an old shoe, a bottle, an oddly shaped loaf of bread, an apple with a fork stuck in it—though rendered with the utmost realism is hardly recognizable, as a result of the extraordinary nature of the lighting which, acting on the colors, makes them overlap forms, the result being nothing short of a chromatic cataclysm.

But despite his studied aloofness Miró could not remain indifferent to the march of events and his *magnum opus* of 1937 was the mural he made for the Spanish Pavilion at the Paris Exposition. This large work, *The Reaper*, figured alongside Picasso's *Guernica* and Calder's mercury fountain, and the three formed an unforgettable ensemble. The panels of *The Reaper* have been lost and this is all the more regrettable because it gave Miró the idea of appealing to a wider public: the idea expressed in his article contributed to *XXe Siècle* (see Appendix 2) under the suggestive title, *I dream of a Big Studio*. It was in this spirit that somewhat later he applied himself to mastering the techniques of pottery and inventing new ones lending themselves to monumental figurations.

On the same support as *The Reaper* (panels of celotex, compressed straw, whose finely corrugated surface provided a "natural" ground) he made some paintings resembling those of 1936 on masonite, but with a more allusive, less overt calligraphy. Faint lines, subdued colors and scumblings serve to evoke gracefully poetic images: *Swallow, Bird Song in Autumn, The Circus, Smoke*. They remind us of the gouache and water-color techniques Miró was then employing in a series of small, highly emotive works. In the large triptych in the Madame Cuttoli Collection Miró reproduces the essentials of these forms, giving them more clarity and precision.

During the winter of 1937-1938 he devoted much time to a new line of research, making elaborate pencil drawings of his face reflected in a mirror. On the extraordinary self-portrait in the James T. Soby Collection, New Canaan, Conn., Miró, working like a man possessed, lavished all the forms that had been haunting his imagination for many years past, and the canvas is covered with a tracery of fine-spun lines fanning out in all directions. Unable to bring himself to paint over the superb design, he confined himself to coloring some of the highlights and the ground spangled with star-like forms. This self-portrait is perhaps the most elaborately constructed of all his works and twenty years were to pass before he completed it. This he did by tracing an exact reproduction of the drawing on another canvas, then superimposing a far-flung arabesque, synthesizing the entire composition.

In 1938 Miró alternated between works involving a gradual return to his world of light, fantastic forms, and his last "wild" paintings (*Head of a Woman*, *Group of People* and the *Seated Woman* in the Peggy Guggenheim Collection) whose frenzied inward drive is evidenced by fantastic distortions, ever-encroaching zones of black, and colors in a state of fusion. The group of *Portraits* dated May-June 1938 forms a sort of transition between two seemingly incongruous conceptions. In *Portrait I* (Baltimore Museum) the composition is dramatic, colors are blurred and broken, and the general effect is still one of sheer ferocity. The texture of the second and third *Portraits* (Kunsthaus, Zurich) is much lighter, and they are based on balanced arrangements of pure colors. In *Portrait IV* (Thompson Collection, Pittsburgh) he reverted to a more intricate composition consisting of variations on a simple theme, a half-length figure telling out on an "astral" landscape. The head hovers above the body, both having approximately equivalent masses. Isolated from rather than linked to the body by a thin thread and slightly tilted back, it exhibits minute signs indicative of the face. The exterior elements, after being integrated into the body, are now dispersed around it. Thus in the "Portraits" sequence we can follow the successive stages by which Miró was now to arrive at his definitive style.

THE BEAUTIFUL BIRD REVEALING THE UNKNOWN TO A PAIR OF LOVERS, 1941.
COLLECTION, THE MUSEUM OF MODERN ART, NEW YORK.

SIGNS IN THE HEAVENS

> Dew diamonds on a spider's web...
> MAX JACOB

VARENGEVILLE, on the Channel coast, once a rallying point of the Surrealists, was in the years 1938-1940 to play the same part in Miró's life and work as that which had been played over so many years by Montroig. "It was under these same far-flung, softly radiant skies that, some thirteen years earlier, two works which clarified and consolidated the 'tone' of Surrealist writing had been conceived: *Traité du Style* and *Nadja*." This passage occurs in the admirable text by André Breton which figures in the album, published by Pierre Matisse in 1959, containing the stencilled reproductions of twenty-two pictures named "Constellations." Planned and partly executed at Varengeville, they were completed by the artist in Palma and Montroig.

Painted in gouache and oils thinned with turpentine on sheets of paper all of the same size (15 by 18 inches, or 18 by 15), these are perhaps the most intricate, most elaborately developed of all Miró's compositions. The "Constellations" form an organic whole, smoothly progressing from each picture to the next without the least break or change of mood, their prevailing atmosphere seemingly quite unaffected by the momentous happenings in the outside world.

In 1938 the architect Nelson who owned a house at Varengeville, lent it to the artist off and on. In 1939 Miró discovered a
small house to let, "Le Clos des Sansonnets," and moved into
it with his family. In this tranquil village on the coast of Normandy, he found a welcome change of surroundings and a
perfect setting for airy flights of the imagination. Houses and
gardens, perched on the brow of the cliffs, overlooked the pale
sea-spaces far below and the moist, lush foliage harmonized
with the shimmering vastness of the Norman skies.

In July 1939 Miró made a first group of pictures on the
theme of *A Bird in Flight above the Plain*. The idea came to him
when he was in the train on the way from Paris to Normandy
and, looking out, had a view of the Vexin plain, with big
crows flying above the bare tilled fields. This visual experience
he synthesized to superb effect; we see the bird upright, soaring
against the wind, while the furrows are indicated by parallel
lines, vertical and horizontal, traversing the picture surface.

When war was declared Miró kept severely to himself, and
immersed himself in his work, firmly refusing to take any active
part in the course of events. (In any case this was the period of
"phoney war" and there were no events to speak of.) Once again
we see a firm resolve to organize the composition, keeping
each element under strict control. To this phase belong two
series of pictures, one on red grounds, the other on burlap
whose hue and texture he left apparent, as though to create an
effect of space, even when using an already existent surface.
For this last, particularly striking and successful group of
pictures, made in November and December 1939, Miró employed
a technique which evidently appealed to him since he often
reverted to it. This was to leave as they were the rough, frayed
edges of the sackcloth. The granulations of the ground were
accentuated by a sort of crushing, that gave them a slight
opaqueness, helping to bring out the play of whitish patches

WOMAN, BIRD, STAR, 1942. INDIAN INK, GOUACHE AND PASTEL.
PRIVATE COLLECTION, GENEVA.

and transparences above. Forms tell boldly out: a woman, a bird, a butterfly and other large confronted insects. These latter are on the point of undergoing a metamorphosis into "signs" but are still in the state of oddly shaped chrysalides. There is a hint of cruelty in these forms, palliated however by the perfect drawing, the gaiety of the pure, elegantly placed colors, and above all by a saving grace of humor.

Like the child who refuses to divert his gaze from some aspect of the world that fascinates him (perhaps so as not to see the others), Miró now seems held by a strange enchantment, his color harmonies have a new resonance, vibrations that linger on and on; his rhythms grow all-pervasive, forms are duplicated to begin with, then multiplied *ad infinitum*. One has an impression that space itself is, so to say, dematerialized, undulating before our eyes. Here the use of paper as the support permits of the most varied nuances, translucencies and scumblings, and, since it does not absorb the pigments, gives full play to their luminosity. Here and there small, black, flashing forms evoke a shower of meteors or stars (in photographic negative) deployed upon a cloudless sky. Such are the "Constellations".

It is only by studying the series as a whole that we can follow the logical, not to say geometrical progress of this galaxy of forms. The first of the series is dated January 20, 1940 and the last September 12, 1941, and there is no break of continuity. The tragic events then taking place in the outside world are not reflected by any interruption of the orderly progression from each composition to the next or of the unity of the cycle. Ten of them were painted at Varengeville while the German army was advancing into France. Then, abruptly, as if awakening from a dream, Miró took the last train available to Paris, accompanied by his family. The "exodus" was already in full swing, but they managed to board a train to Spain. His friend Prats came to meet him at Gerona, and succeeded in booking a passage for

WOMAN AND BIRD BEFORE THE MOON, 1944. PRIVATE COLLECTION.

him to Palma de Mallorca, where he was welcomed by his wife's family. On August 1 Miró started painting again, taking up his work where he had dropped it and, seemingly unaffected by the turn of events across the frontier, kept resolutely to the program he had set himself. He completed the "Constellations" sequence at Montroig in autumn 1941.

In an interview with James J. Sweeney (*Partisan Review*, February 1948) Miró spoke of the pictures of this series as having been "exacting both technically and physically... A few forms suggested here would call for other forms elsewhere to

WOMAN IN THE NIGHT, 1945. PIERRE MATISSE GALLERY, NEW YORK.

WOMEN IN THE NIGHT, 1945. GALERIE MAEGHT, PARIS.

balance them. These in turn developed others." He goes on to describe the "full and complex equilibrium" he now was trying to attain and adds that "night, music and the stars" began to play a major part in suggesting the form and content of these pictures. And, in the result, these elements continued to be dominating factors in his work for several years. When he was in Palma he would sit for hours in the dim light of the cathedral listening to the organ, musing, lost in dreams.

The counterpoint of elements deriving from earth and sky in the "Constellations" is of a highly personal and peculiar description, all being joined together by lines of force, an elaborate network of cyclic rhythms and "gyres," adjusted with geometrical precision to the overall compositional scheme. The technique Miró invented to match up to this program has been described by André Breton as "his highly ingenious device of splashing with vivid light only the points of intersection of lines" and "a luminous accentuation of the menisci created by interactions of concrete and abstract elements." Color is put to the service of form in terms of a strictly-applied organizational formula; thus, as Jacques Dupin has pointed out, "whenever a black star cuts through a red disk, the part of the surface common to both is always yellow." It may seem strange that in the course of these two years Miró produced only some twenty pictures, but we must bear in mind the tremendous effort of concentration that was needed to achieve and maintain at the same level the creative tension involved in making this sequence of intricate, perfectly balanced compositions, in which the artist demonstrates a supreme mastery of the picture surface and of spatial recession. The successive works of the series reveal a coherent, if not strictly logical, development; while aligned to an initial overall conception, they assume different orientations whenever a new group of forms emerges and proliferates.

The first "Constellations" are still peopled with large, recognizable figures and certain dominant celestial bodies. Next, the rhythms begin to oscillate, the lines start moving and, interlocking, weave a sort of spider's web (a term that figures in the name of one of these pictures). Distinctively geometric signs become more frequent, while, concurrently, the oddly shaped human figures dwindle in size, the result being a relative equivalence between the various picture elements, human, celestial or wholly invented by the artist. Some motifs, however, for example the ladder, persistently recur. Sometimes, too—like the animals on the walls of prehistoric caves—the human figures are confronted by a singular array of traps, magic signs, arrows and stars.

The colors, few in number, have an amazing clarity and potency, and no less vivid are the small areas of black disposed with extreme precision at carefully chosen points. Their combination produces an effect of kaleidoscopic, meticulously ordered diversity. All are bathed in a nocturnal light or a dim phosphorescent sheen like the effect produced by a faintly illuminated stage when the curtain rises.

The names given by Miró to these successive glimpses of a world beyond the world reveal both the organic unity of his ideas and his passionate desire to open up new fields of vision. In a survey of his œuvre as a whole we note a curious anomaly; sometimes the titles of his pictures are vague, signifying nothing definite, and sometimes, on the other hand, they have a fine poetic precision. The latter is true of the group we now are dealing with. Whereas he sometimes shows a tendency to verbalize in titles assigned to other works, those he gives his "Constellations" have an enchanting, almost Blakian naivety: *The Ladder of Escape, The Nightingale's Song at Midnight and Morning Rain, On the 13th the Ladder Touched the Firmament, The Poetess, Waking at Daybreak, Women on the Shore of a Lake made Iridescent by a Passing Swan, The Passage of the Divine Bird.*

Though few in number, these finely constructed works contain between them an amazing wealth and variety of forms. Indeed they furnished Miró with a complete repertory of images on which he was to draw persistently in the coming years, not only for the multitude of gouaches, watercolors and drawings in which, after a period of self-imposed privation, he gave free course to his creative zest, but also for the large murals he made in the United States soon after.

On settling down again in Barcelona in 1942, he applied himself, to start with, to a series of small works, remarkable for the freedom of their conception and execution, in which he gave a new prominence to details from the "Constellations" sequence. The special significance of each motif treated as an isolated unit is clearly indicated by gestures, features and accessories, which though still on occasion faintly sinister, are oftener whimsical and gay. The techniques employed by Miró in these small pictures are both novel and ingenious; powdered pastel, charcoal, Indian ink, gouache and watercolors on a paper support. Flakes of pure color and various shades of black stand out on an iridescent ground, traversed by broken gleams. Some of these experimental procedures suggest that Miró was now beginning to feel attracted by the possibilities of engraving and fully plastic form. Indeed he was already testing out new procedures in ceramics. His first were produced in collaboration with his friend Artigas, a highly skillful potter, whom he had known for many years.

It was not until 1944 that Miró reverted to easel painting; to begin with, pictures of small dimensions, in which he transposed on to canvas with remarkable precision and sureness of hand, forms he had invented for the experimental works described above. Usually he employed light grounds; occasionally quite plain or very slightly tinted canvas. The motifs here are of a purely calligraphic order and of a quite original type; sometimes they are enhanced at "strategic" points by flecks of pure color. Sometimes, too, he includes passages of simulated wear-and-tear both in the grounds and in the signs. Soon (in 1945) he takes to using larger formats, but the composition retains its ethereal lightness. Forms, however, are delineated with

WOMEN LISTENING TO MUSIC, 1945. COLLECTION HANS NEUMANN, CARACAS.

the utmost clarity, and the colors, serving an essentially graphic purpose, act merely as an accompaniment. In some of these pictures Miró leaves certain parts of the canvas in its natural color and uses them as backgrounds for the operative signs. These "islands" of white are surrounded by vast black areas

PAINTING, 1949. COLLECTION OF MR AND MRS RALPH F. COLIN, NEW YORK.

THE GLARE OF THE SUN WOUNDING THE LATE STAR, 1951.
GUSTAV ZUMSTEG COLLECTION, ZURICH.

upon which prolongations of the lines are inscribed in white. Have we here reminiscences of the long hours he spent in the dim light of the cathedral, which he always associated with the sound of music? The names certainly suggest this: *Women listening to Music, A Ballet Dancer listening to Organ Music in a Gothic Cathedral.*

MURAL PAINTING FOR THE GRADUATE CENTER OF HARVARD UNIVERSITY.

Despite Miró's long stay in Spain, which now was drawing to an end, he was far from being forgotten in Paris. Fifty recent works of his were published in *Cahiers d'Art* (1946) and he was given a prominent place in the International Surrealist Exhibition of 1947 at the Galerie Maeght, the same place he had been accorded in the 1938 Surrealist Exhibition at the Galerie des Beaux-Arts. Indeed his position as a leader of the movement had remained unchallenged throughout the decade. But meanwhile he had become a celebrity in the United States, where

1950-1951. PIERRE MATISSE GALLERY. NEW YORK.

many European painters had taken refuge during the war years and there had been a great upsurge of artistic creativity. Pierre Matisse's active championship of Miró and his success in getting works by him taken by the most eminent collectors had borne fruit and at the end of 1941 the first retrospective exhibition of his pictures took place at the Museum of Modern Art. On this occasion Mr James J. Sweeney published, along with the catalogue, an excellent monograph on the artist and followed this up with several authoritative articles in reviews. In 1945

95

Pierre Matisse exhibited the "Constellations" and Miró's first ceramics. In 1947, having been given a commission to paint a large mural for the Gourmet Restaurant of the Terrace Plaza Hotel in Cincinnati, Miró proceeded to America.

After carefully inspecting the wall surface allotted to 'his mural—it faced a circular bay giving on the open air—he rented a large studio in New York City and started work. In this painting, over ten yards in length, he included all the basic themes of the pictures he had been working on in recent years, arranging them lengthwise in a continuous frieze. Surprise has sometimes been expressed at the fact that there is no essential difference between his murals and his easel pictures. The reason for this is that his oil paintings and even the gouaches and sketches leading up to them were conceived in terms of the wall space they might occupy, whatever their dimensions. Thus their linear structure lends itself to the most drastic enlargement; moreover, even in his colors Miró displays a remarkable flexibility particularly suited to the demands of wall painting.

Fortified by this experience, Miró made his mural for the dining-room of the Graduate Center at Harvard. Subsequently, in view of the risks of deterioration to which this majestic work was exposed *in situ*, it was moved to a museum and its place taken by a large ceramic panel. These murals prove that Miró is one of the painters who has best understood present-day architecture, in which empty spaces count as much as full ones and the distribution of the structural elements in space creates the volumes. Miró does not set out to decorate or disguise the wall, but to bring it to life by inserting at vital points sources of light and foci of interest. This enables him to animate very large surfaces without producing any effect either of dispersion or of monotony. Indeed by its very nature his painting has much in common with architecture, neither vying with it nor subservient, but joining forces with it on an equal footing.

RECREATING NATURE

Vite une tranche de terre
Vite une tranche de feu
Car la nuit arrive
Avec sa mèche de sang.

JEAN ARP

DURING his first stay in the United States Miró was chiefly concerned with studying the reactions of such old friends as Marcel Duchamp, Calder, Tanguy and J. L. Sert to the experiments he had been making in the years of self-imposed reclusion. Yet he was keenly alive to the ambience of the great city, the glaring lights of Broadway and the strenuous material and psychological conditions of life in the New World. And his art was soon to show the effects of these experiences.

Miró returned to Paris in 1948 and when, at the Galerie Maeght, he exhibited his recent work, his many friends—painters, writers and critics—were all enthusiasm. In 1949 a retrospective exhibition took place at Bern, then another at Basel, and in the following year yet another exhibition (one hundred and thirty works) at the Galerie Maeght. Meanwhile he was engaged on two large sets of illustrations, the etchings begun in New York in Atelier 17, directed by the British painter and engraver Hayter, for Tristan Tzara's *Antitête*, and a set of lithographs for the same author's *Parler Seul*. During these two years he also made a large number of paintings in his studios at Barcelona and Montroig.

Miró has a habit of making sequences of paintings similar in kind, then switching over, every two or three years (or more), to works conceived in a quite different spirit; sometimes painting with meticulous precision, sometimes giving scope to an instinctual drive accompanied by outbursts of explosive violence. Now however, he followed both paths at once, making on the one hand elaborate, carefully thought-out compositions (his so-called "slow paintings") and, on the other, completely spontaneous works in which he cast off all restraint, incorporated the most unlikely substances, often mere detritus, in his pigment and applied the color in patches or "unpremeditated smears." The nearer his painting approaches a certain standard of perfection, the finality of a last word, the more uneasy Miró feels about it. Indeed no sooner has he seen a project through to its conclusion than he feels an urge to make a clean sweep and start afresh. And soon a recourse to other disciplines gave him a pretext for launching out yet again on a new venture.

Distinctive of the "slow" paintings is the extreme attention given to building up the grounds, which contain a wide range of light, finely modulated colors passing from mauve to green, from red to grey, and, acting as a luminous backcloth, lend warmth to the composition. Then, once the whole surface has been suffused with color, figures are indicated exclusively by oppositions of black and white, to which are sometimes added a few clear-cut touches of pure color. Always elegantly balanced, whether isolated or juxtaposed, they have an effect of floating in a sea of fiery light.

The "unpremeditated" paintings, on the other hand, give an impression of having been dashed off on the spur of the moment. Working at high speed, the painter strews the canvas with indistinct touches of color and strokes slashed on so violently as to rule out pentimenti, and he has no qualms about integrating all sorts of foreign substances. Yet perhaps the two methods are

BIRD WITH A CALM GAZE, ITS WINGS AFLAME, 1952.
MOLTZAU COLLECTION, OSLO.

not really so incongruous. We can see that Miró is feeling a need to stiffen up his painting and give it density. He has recourse to his time-proved procedures as well as to adventures of free fancy, and experiments with the most heterogeneous materials, "transmuting" them with the sleight of an alchemist of genius.

99

In the large body of work dating to 1952-1953 Miró achieves a satisfying fusion of the seemingly incompatible trends described above. His line, which had run a risk of dessication in the rarefied atmosphere of a pure linearism, now finds sustenance in the thickness of the reliefs in which it is inscribed. An example is the *Bird with a Calm Gaze, its Wings Aflame.* Broadly delineated, the figures have a four-square solidity, a massiveness that is relieved only by the slender threads linking them to tiny symbols rendered with characteristically fine precision. Sometimes, as in the large painting of 1953 in the Solomon R. Guggenheim Museum, New York, the operative lines are implemented by one or more rows of colored dots, at once emphasizing contours and giving them luminous fringes like those of the leather marionettes of Indonesia and Turkey.

Acquiring a mobility and a life of their own, forms develop into boldly stated entities—suns, stars, exclamation marks—or are converted into supple arabesques enveloping the subject and suggesting by variations in their thickness its consistency and volume. In the latter case the brightly colored backgrounds

◀ PAINTING, 1952. PIERRE MATISSE GALLERY, NEW YORK.

PAINTING, 1953. PHILIPPE DOTREMONT COLLECTION, UCCLE (BRUSSELS).

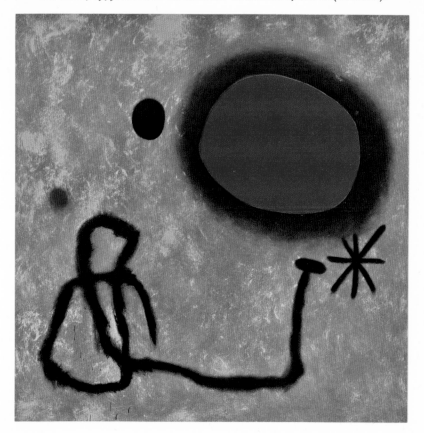

101

are strewn with large black or near-black elemental signs, ideograms that arrest the gaze but often, like primitive hiero-glyphics, seem to defy interpretation. These strange forms, instinct with magic potency, have appropriate formats, being painted on tall, narrow doors or long scroll-like friezes.

Though in 1954-1955 Miró still produced some pictures in his latest manner (chiefly violent, deliberately graceless works), we feel that this source of inspiration was tending to run dry and the execution becoming less felicitous. The reason for the change was that he was now absorbed in exploring the resources of a new technique and its applications to the rendering of forms, surfaces and volumes. Its problems and possibilities intrigued and fascinated him, and he was now to devote several years to intensive research on these lines, for he was convinced that this venture into a new field of action would open up vast horizons and lead to discoveries of a wholly novel order.

What Miró had in mind was not a readjustment of any traditional technique of painting or a new mode of decoration, but a resort to methods used by primitive man in making painted and carved forms, and the choice and elaboration of such materials as lent themselves to these. We must not forget that many years before, in the heyday of Surrealism, Miró had developed a taste for trying out new substances in his paintings, and had also formed a habit of studying objects chance threw in his way and assembling them in meaningful figurations. He has always been a collector of what Surrealists call *objets trouvés*, not for their rarity or intrinsic value, but for the "state of grace" or "revelations" he sometimes finds in them. Now that at long last he possesses in Majorca the "big studio" he dreamt of, he can surround himself with the treasure trove of his country walks: driftwood, pebbles polished by the waves, seashells, old horseshoes, worn-out, discarded farmyard imple-ments. He likes them for the same reason that he likes objects of daily use and artefacts of the popular imagination, and he draws inspiration from them exactly as they are. For unlike some of his surrealist friends he does not try to interpret or improve these objects, or to tamper with the "personalities" they have acquired as the result of neglect or wear and tear. Gazing at them, he detects curious analogies suggestive of new forms, which set him in the mood to work—as when a gourd mounted on two sticks conjures up the image of a bird.

Most of the combinations of such objects made in the surrealist period (some of which were exhibited) have disappeared owing to the fragility of the materials employed. Miró now applied himself to the problem of ensuring the survival of his creations in this field and, in the years 1945-1950, tried his hand at modeling in clay small figures with squat, rudimentary forms like those of primitive female idols; also, heads and bird-forms reminiscent of the anthropomorphic vases of early cultures. A dozen or so of these figurines were cast in terracotta or bronze. Pottery gave him opportunities both for more original creations and for carrying through with his own hands the molding of these imagined forms and concrete objects.

His early ventures in this field dated back to 1944-1946, but the great creative period fell between 1954 and 1960. Miró's instructor in this technique and, thereafter, collaborator in his experiments and joint creator of the major works of this later phase, was his old friend Joseph Llorens Artigas. In two articles published in *Derrière le Miroir* (Nos. 87-89, June-August 1956) Artigas describes the successive stages of their collaboration. In 1942 Miró, who had been greatly struck by the ceramics exhibited by Artigas at Barcelona, had some difficulty in persuading his friend to let him work as his assistant. To test Miró's seriousness, Artigas assigned to him the most thankless tasks. "His application, his staying power and his prompt reactions to the accidents inevitable in firing overcame any scruples I had felt about accepting his proposal... This was the beginning of a close collaboration in which I now saw boundless possibilities for the future. Miró's creative imagination is simply prodigious and, though I had no 'professional' bias against the gifted amateur, it was up to me, as a technician, to steer clear of the pitfalls which, owing to his temerity, we encountered at every step." Between them Miró and his friend produced ten large vases in the 1940s as well as many decorative plaques. This experience had shown how fruitful their cooperation could be and pointed the way to a joint venture on a larger scale, in which the two men pooled their resources.

It was of this that Miró was thinking one evening in 1950 when he said to Artigas: "We must have another go at ceramics, you and I. All our painters are setting up as potters nowadays, but most of them miss the mark pretty badly. The reason is that they go on painting in the usual way, without a thought for the special nature of the medium they are handling, the enamels, colors, etc.—indeed the whole spirit of ceramic art. As regards forms, the most they do is to risk some mild distortions. It's high time for us to take action." As it so happened, Artigas left Barcelona next year (1951) and bought a house in the ancient Pyrenean village of Gallifa; there he installed an exceptionally large kiln with an eye to the works he had in mind.

When he went to visit his friend at Gallifa, Miró was struck by the similarity of the countryside, all in rugged crags and woodlands, to that of the Sierras he roamed in his boyhood. Several months were spent in passionate discussion of Miró's project; however it was not until 1953, after Artigas had thoroughly examined the composite objects Miró had been making for years, that they tackled the problem of converting works of this type into ceramics. Abandoning the idea of casting them (this would have lessened the vitality of the originals), they decided to make ceramic *equivalents* of the very diverse materials

STELE, 1955-1956. CERAMIC. GALERIE MAEGHT, PARIS.

FIGURE, 1955. CERAMIC. GALERIE MAEGHT, PARIS.

employed. Joan, Artigas's son, who was just starting to learn the potter's craft and had no preconceived ideas on the subject, was called in to assist. They began by making large steles and stone blocks whose shapes were suggested by natural rock-formations; then they moved on to pebbles and "eggs" of various sizes. When keeping to traditional type-forms—vases, dishes, bowls—they made all sorts of additions, not only completely altering their normal aspects but also necessitating their employment for unwonted, non-utilitarian purposes. Soon Miró had mastered the potter's technique so thoroughly that he was able to create forms entirely of his own invention, owing nothing to any model. The baking of these pieces began in 1954. Next came the glazing. With each successive firing, Miró lit on new ideas, made technical improvements and obtained better results. Each piece was worked over several times and underwent several firings, sometimes as many as eight. One has the impression of a constant struggle between the natural inertia of the material and the unforeseeable changes produced by the accidents of baking. On May 10, 1956 the last batch went to the oven. Two hundred and thirty-two pieces were crated and sent to Paris, where they were exhibited at the Galerie Maeght.

Visitors to that exhibition will never forget the unique sensation they experienced on entering this forest of strange forms, petrified yet mysteriously alive, and of an almost tropical luxuriance. The brilliancy of these porous materials charged with light and color, enriched with glazes, sand and gleaming pebbles, was like a revelation of a whole new world of beauty. For cooking with wood fires enables effects unobtainable with gas, charcoal or electricity. In the larger, monumental structures Miró combined elements baked separately. Examples of this method are the *Totems* and the *Portico*, containing nine ceramic elements, now in the Solomon R. Guggenheim Museum, New York. Miró found scope for his playful wit in smaller pieces

HEAD, 1956. CERAMIC. GALERIE MAEGHT, PARIS.

SELF-PORTRAIT, 1937-1960. GALERIE MAEGHT, PARIS.

with grotesque excrescences, whimsical proliferations. Utterly unlike any other form of art, these objects have a shock effect, a palpable, startling impact, on the beholder.

"While working together," Artigas tells us, "we soon realized that we were invading the domain of architecture, making facings for walls, or independent elements and objects having an architectural application." In 1955 UNESCO's Art Committee asked Miró to participate in the decoration of its new buildings on the Place Fontenoy in Paris. The surfaces he was commissioned to decorate were two walls three meters high, one fifteen meters long, the other seven and a half. Both walls were out in the open, facing the Lecture Room. Miró decided to make the decoration entirely in ceramic, in collaboration with Artigas. While planning this work with reference to the building as a whole, he aimed at striking a contrast with it, as he explained in an article in *Derrière le Miroir* (Nos. 107-109, 1958). "Thus as a counterpoise to the huge concrete slabs surrounding it, the idea occurred to me that a large, bright red disk should figure on the larger wall. Its counterpart on the small wall would be provided by a blue crescent, adjusted to the more restricted, more intimate space for which it was intended... Specific elements of the building, such as the placing of the windows, suggested the checkered composition and the shapes of the human figures. I aimed at brutal expression in the big wall, and a more poetic one in the smaller." So as to make sure that large plaques of this order, exposed to the elements without any protection, yet capable of "taking" glazes and colors, should stand up to the Paris climate, Artigas began by making a long series of experiments with the materials available. The two friends inspected the famous paleolithic wall paintings at Altamira, the Romanesque frescoes in the Barcelona Museum and Gaudi's decorations. And an old wall at Santillana gave them the idea of replacing the uniform plaques they had hitherto used by

THREE BIRDS IN SPACE, 1938-1960. GALERIE MAEGHT, PARIS.

SWALLOW DAZZLED BY THE GLARE OF THE RED PUPIL, 1925-1960.
JANLET COLLECTION, BRUSSELS.

others irregularly shaped and having more vitality. For their purpose was to build a wall of colors, not merely to adorn an existing structure. Simultaneously executed, both forms and colors were spread out on the ground with a broom composed of palm-tree fibre, and kept intact the dynamism of the initial impulse. By general consent this was the most successful and original of all the decorations of the UNESCO headquarters. It was for this work that Miró was awarded the Guggenheim Prize in 1958.

In the summer of 1960 he created another ceramic on a monumental scale; this was to replace his 1951 mural at Harvard, transferred to the Fogg Art Museum. There was of course no question of remaking the painting of ten years earlier in another medium. His style and execution had made great forward strides and needless to say he kept to the disciplines of the new technique he had mastered so thoroughly. This time he worked on plaques of uniform dimensions forming a panel inset in the wall. It was in the handling of the *matière* that Miró displayed the greatest boldness; attacking his subject forthrightly and spontaneously, without a preliminary maquette, and in a broader linear technique (inspired also by his experiences in etching and lithography), he built up large primitive figures. Some accents of pure color stand out on a ground of powdered vitreous pigment. Like the born potter he is, Miró has an almost uncanny prescience of the exact effect firing will have on his colors.

This evolution of his art, so deeply pondered over in its inception, now proceeds automatically, one could almost say autonomously. And it seems to be leading him across the frontier of a new universe. When Miró recommenced painting in 1959, the richly rewarding experiences of the preceding period led him to instill a wholly spontaneous, lyrical effusion into his pictorial technique. Delineated (as always) with an incomparable sureness of hand, his forms tell out in an ever more tenuous, more ethereal atmosphere. His painting continues its gestation and maturation, like a wild plant released from the gardener's control. This may account in some measure for the bewilderment of those who visited the two 1961 exhibitions of his recent work at the Galerie Maeght, the second of which was reserved to very large paintings done in the spirit of murals.

Miro 50

MURAL PAINTING III, 1962.
OWNED BY THE ARTIST.

During the years when Miró was working on ceramics, usually in Artigas's home at Gallifa, he had had a house with the "big studio" of his dreams built for him at Palma de Mallorca. He had severed all his links with Barcelona and created a new setting for his life and work, in which he now could feast his eyes on vast expanses of sky and sea. To make this new house seem more homelike, he filled it with familiar household gods, all the objects and materials he had been collecting indefatigably for many years. He also took this opportunity of studying the contents of his portfolios, drawings and souvenirs, and in so doing discovered canvases he had forgotten, works he had started and then dropped. Among the abandoned projects were some that seemed worth re-interpreting from a new angle.

The works he now harked back to were of two kinds. First, those of his "poetic" period, whose possibilities, he saw, had by no means been exhausted, notably as regards his renderings of atmospheric effects and vaporous surfaces with luminous signs, like nebulae, gleaming through the ambient darkness. Then, again, he scrutinized the eerie figurations of the years of unrest, obsessive presences he then was trying to exorcise and unclear accretions for which, in the light of his new knowledge, he now saw simplified equivalents. Here we have an explanation of his drastic modifications of the 1938 self-portrait. Two large black hieroglyphs stand out upon the color, and soon he replaces this too and confines himself to inserting tenuous graffiti of lightly sprayed color on a misty, almost hueless ground. Greatly daring, he is breaking away from his most firmly rooted preconceptions and, guided by an inner logic, arriving at an art of vast, very faintly tinted surfaces on which figures only a tiny sign, a delicately modulated line like that of a distant melody played on a shepherd's flute. And in this primeval, pastoral landscape Miró bides his time, silently awaiting tomorrow's miracles, his fingers to his lips.

APPENDICES

We here reproduce writings and statements made by Miró in his early days;
also texts which are sometimes quoted
in part, but which, having appeared in
periodicals prior to 1939, are rarely
accessible in their complete form.

PREFACE TO THE 1921 MIRÓ EXHIBITION
AT THE GALERIE LA LICORNE, PARIS

by Maurice Raynal

Like perfumes, youth manifests itself, as a rule, under two different forms, a natural one and an artificial. This also applies to art, which has its nature-lovers and its enemies of nature. Some young artists prefer to operate "in a state of nature," with both their talents and their blemishes left plain to see, while others prefer to wear collars and elegantly cut, "slenderizing" costumes. The former ask no more than to carry out the task nature has assigned them; whereas young artists of the second kind deliberately turn their back on nature and make a point of camouflaging (as they hope) the shortcomings of their early efforts with all sorts of tricks of the trade. These latter make the mistake of beginning at the end; true, they sometimes succeed in producing showy little works that have the air of masterpieces, of a kind, but when one looks into them more closely they prove to be no more than desperate attempts on the artist's part to outreach his grasp, and all too often give an impression that there is little prospect he will ever advance beyond this stage. In the case of the young artists of the other class, we can sense, even in their juvenile fumblings, even in their downright blunders, qualities that are eminently perfectible, qualities which, with wider experience, seconded by native skill, will blossom forth, as if by magic, when the moment comes.

Joan Miró is of this latter type; he has the gift of what can only be described as purity, the natural freshness which, if not quite immune from that skin-disease of young persons known as acne, has the supreme merit of being wholly exempt from cosmetics, those artificial aids to "beauty" to which stripling art is all too prone to have recourse.

In this youthful discretion we can see, no doubt, the influence of that sage adviser Dalmau, who is sending Miró to us from Barcelona, at just the right moment, neither too soon nor too late.

Better still, Miró does not flaunt on his escutcheon some armorial device before having won his spurs, nor has he qualms about employing objects already used by his forbears. As you will see, he often drinks in the cup of grandfather Cézanne, and smokes the pipe of uncle Picasso, though this does not lead him to disdain the frolics of his quaintly illuminated rocking-horse or the animals in the sheepfold of his childhood.

Here, obviously, we have hall-marks of the most assured unsureness —but what defect of youth can be more charming! One thing is clear, however, even in this early phase; from the way he has treated his portrait we can be sure that never will Miró allow sentimentality to submerge his overriding interest in the play *per se* of forms and colors.

In this context we may draw attention to a fact that is important for its bearing on Miró's art: the fact that clashes often develop among the forms and colors he sets out to reconcile and that he does not always make peace between them. Here, instead of weighing the respective claims, the judge starts wrangling with the lawyers—not so bad a method as it seems, provided the judge knows his business. Anyhow, when dealing with a temperament nourished by a truly fertile imagination, why linger over technicalities? This much is clear: that, gifted as he is, Miró is by way of opening new fields to the creative imagination. He has any amount of courage, but a courage that is never provocative. Sometimes he may seem foolhardy, but is not foolhardiness a frequent attribute of courage, and is it not also a source of those fruitful errors which have time and again served art's advancement? Moreover, it is just when Miró is at his boldest that he produces his most satisfying pictures, and it is in the works in which this quality is given freest play that we best discern the personality of a painter who has already made good his claim to be a pioneer.

The fact is, too, that Miró's sensibility is still guided by an elementary notion common to many youthful artists: the notion that leads the child and the primitive to jotting here and there on the canvas or sheet of paper the elements of their preliminary sketches, without attempting to fuse them into a coherent whole. None the less we can feel that already he is struggling to master the rules of composition, though this discipline still tends to go against the grain and his urge to fancy-free creation.

It would also seem that by way of the juvenile ardor, coupled with a rather touching inexpertness that pervades these works, Miró is trying to relieve his sensibility of an oppressive burden, and to choose the loudest words with which he can give expression to it. One cannot expect of so young an artist the sureness of touch that comes of long experience; hence these vociferations, these seemingly reckless acrobatics. Yet an understanding observer will surely grasp the purport of these manifestations of a sensibility that has not yet felt a need to set its house in order.

There is another peculiarity of Miró's art that is an outcome of this overriding sensibility. Like his compatriot Don Juan, he is moved by a well-nigh indiscriminate love, and all the motifs of the visible surge up under his hand, once his sensitivity comes into action. And handicapped by his desire to embrace them all, he fails to grasp them to his satisfaction. Lacking the capacity of seducing them methodically one by one, he loses heart and patience, caresses them and drops them, then in feverish haste turns to them again, but only, as a rule, to shatter them to pieces. None the less, such is Miró's artistry, the fragments that survive are excellent and, even if he often kills the hen to get the egg, we can enjoy lunching with him on the former.

But Miró has not yet got all he wants out of these ventures; there are times indeed when he seems appalled by the carnage he has perpetrated. With the result that when his highly-strung sensibility fails to find an object measuring up to its requirements, he sometimes has to count on himself alone to give expression to his pent-up, unshared emotions, and falls back either on his imagination (slightly diverted, as a result, from its natural path) or his keen personal interest in the physical process of painting so as to find a means of assuaging—so to say artificially—his headstrong impulse to a perfection still beyond his reach.

This, again, is an experience we have all gone through, to some extent: the penalty of youthful aspirations.

Footit used to say to his fellow-clown Monsieur Loyal, "Excuse me, Sir, could you tell me where I'm going?" and this is, in effect, the question Miró seems to be putting to his fellow-pilgrims in the world of art which he is now exploring step by cautious step. Here is a tentative answer to this difficult inquiry.

"Yes, my dear Miró, you are living in that happy period in which one doesn't know where one is going or if one's getting there. You are not, so far, convinced of this, but soon enough you'll make a discovery that will open to you the gates of hell and play havoc with your peace of mind. For the moment don't believe a word of all these old wives' tales. That you don't know where you are going matters little; the great thing is to make haste to get there—as you're doing now, and very well. Naturally you would not believe me if I told you that we are donkeys with luscious-looking carrots dangled in front of their noses to make them run. You would shrug your shoulders, and quite rightly, if I told you that people imagine they are wonderfully clever only because they think up satisfactions for needs that they've invented for themselves, or that the only problems they ever solve are those they have themselves created. You're at the happy age when all the bells strike the same note, when one begins a phrase without knowing how it will end, when one says to oneself: 'Let's go ahead and paint; there will always be time, later, to find out what we were driving at!' The only guide you consult—and very wisely too, appearances notwithstanding—is your heart. Quite likely that guide will lead you nowhere, but it will show you the best way of getting there, take my word for it!

"Go ahead, then! You're fit and twenty and have all the means you need to take you far. So run happily after your own shadow. You are convinced you'll catch it. Have it your own way, then, you'll catch it—but how I envy you!"

I DREAM OF A BIG STUDIO
by Joan Miró

In *XXe Siècle*, No. 2, 1938
Reproduced by permission of G. di San Lazzaro

On arriving in Paris, in March, 1919, I took a room in the Hôtel de la Victoire, in Rue Notre-Dame-des-Victoires. After being in Paris all winter I went back to Spain, and stayed in the country. Next winter I came again to Paris and stayed in another hotel, 32 Boulevard Pasteur. It was there that Paul Rosenberg looked me up, Picasso and Maurice Raynal having spoken to him about me. Soon after, Pablo Gargallo who was spending the winter at Barcelona where he was Professor of Sculpture at the School of Fine Arts, let me move into his studio at 45 Rue Blomet, next door to the Bal Nègre which Robert Desnos was later to "discover." André Masson had the studio next to mine, there was only a thin partition between. Then I settled down to work and painted the *Head of a Spanish Dancer* (owned by Picasso), the *Table with Glove*, etc. It was a very hard time for me; the window-panes were broken and my stove, which I'd picked up in the Flea Market, refused to work. Still, the studio was very clean. I did my own housework. As I was so poor I could only pay for one lunch per week; the other days I made do with dried figs and chewing-gum.

Next year Gargallo's studio was not available. I stayed in a small hotel on the Boulevard Raspail and it was there I completed *The Farmer's Wife*, *The Ear of Grain* and some other pictures. Next, I moved into furnished rooms in the Rue Berthollet. *The Carbide Lamp.* Summer in the country. Returned to the studio in the Rue Blomet. Completed *The Farm*, work on which had been begun at Montroig and continued at Barcelona. Léonce Rosenberg, Kahnweiler, Jacques Doucet, all the Surrealists, Pierre Loeb, and Ernest Hemingway came to see me. Hemingway bought *The Farm*. In the Rue Blomet studio I painted *The Harlequin's Carnival* and the *Spanish Dancer* in the Gaffé Collection. Though I was now beginning to sell my pictures it still was rather hard going. For *The Harlequin's Carnival* I made a number of preliminary drawings in which I expressed my hallucinations due to hunger; I came home at night without having dined, and put down my sensations as they came. That year I was much in the company of poets, and I felt I must go beyond the "plastic fact" if I was to achieve poetry.

Some months later Jacques Viot organized my first one-man show, at the Galerie Pierre. After that I had a contract with Viot that enabled me to keep afloat. I rented a studio at the Villa des Fusains (22, Rue Tourlaque), which was formerly used by Lautrec and Derain and where Pierre Bonnard still has his studio. At the time Paul Eluard, Max Ernst, Goemans, a Belgian dealer in the Rue de la Seine, René Magritte and Arp were living there. On the door I stuck a placard I'd picked up in a shop. *Non-stop train passing.* My affairs were looking up a bit, but it was still a struggle; once Arp and I had only radishes and butter for lunch. As soon as I could manage it I took a bigger, ground-floor studio in the Villa, but I did not keep it long.

I went back to Spain, married, returned to Paris with my wife and moved out of the Villa des Fusains (where I had painted a whole series of blue pictures) into an apartment in the Rue François-Mouthon. I did a lot of work and spent most of the year in Spain, where I found it easier to concentrate on what I was doing. When at Barcelona, I worked in the room where I had been born.

But I never had a real studio in Spain though I often went there. To start with, I worked in little cells I could just squeeze into. When I wasn't satisfied with my work I banged my head against the wall! My dream, if and when I can manage to settle down somewhere, is to have a really big studio, not for reasons of lighting, a north light and so forth— these things don't trouble me—but just to have space enough, room for lots of canvases; for the more I work, the more I want to work. I'd like to try my hand at sculpture, pottery, engraving, and to have a private press. Also to try, so far as possible, to advance beyond easel-painting, which in my opinion has a rather paltry message and, by means of painting of another kind, get into closer contact with the masses, whom I have always kept in mind.

At present I am staying in the house, in the Boulevard Blanqui, where Nelson, the architect, lives. It was here that Mrs Hemingway kept *The Farm* before taking it to the U.S.A.

I once thought I'd like to have another look at the studio in Rue Blomet. There was a very fine lilac in the yard. The house was being torn down. A big dog made a dash at me.

Joan Miró.

THE EMANCIPATION OF PAINTING

Miró to Tériade

Minotaure No. 3/4, p. 18

Miró loquitur: It's never easy for me to talk about my painting since it is always born in a state of hallucination induced by some kind of shock, objective or subjective, for which I am not personally responsible in the least. As regards my means of expression, I try my hardest to achieve the maximum of clarity, power and plastic aggressiveness; a physical sensation to begin with, followed up by an impact on the psyche.

WHERE ARE YOU GOING, MIRO?

by Georges Duthuit

Cahiers d'Art, No. 8-10, 1936
Reproduced by permission of Christian Zervos

MIRÓ — Our generation lacks heroism and a deeply revolutionary spirit.

G. D. — Still it seems to me that in Spain...

MIRÓ — I'm keeping strictly to the field of painting.

G. D. — How I'd like to have a field I could rely on!

MIRÓ — Remember the Impressionists; they grew their own potatoes. Then the Cubists...

G. D. — And today?

MIRÓ — Today my young contemporaries put up a good fight so long as they are poor, but once they make ends meet it's another story. How I admire artists like Bonnard or Maillol, so different from those men who in their thirties start hauling down their flag. Bonnard and Maillol will go on fighting till their last breath; each year of their old age brings a new lease of life. Great artists grow in strength, strike out in new directions as the years go by. But what are we to think of those bluffers who, the moment they have a cocktail in hand, a nice thick carpet underfoot and a titled lady to greet them, start bowing and scraping like the tame dogs they are!

G. D. — Weak vessels! It's the same old story. One has to steer clear of, or, rather fight...

MIRÓ — Yes, to fight society, whether it's high or middle class, and to resist every social order, even the new one that's knocking at the door, if it wants to make us kowtow to it. For me, too, the word "freedom" has a meaning and I'll defend it at all costs.

G. D. — That's what they mean by the tragic lot of the artist, I suppose. You talk of "fighting"—where, with whom, and why?

MIRÓ — Not in a well-warmed café, in any case. Not with irresponsible intellectuals; not in defense of their silly theories. Let them go on chewing the empty husks of their abstractions, for lack of any solid food, any facts to go on, any real rhythm, any sense of human actualities.

Have you ever heard of any bigger absurdity than the "pure abstraction" they talk about. And they want me to join them in their empty house! Given the fact that all the signs I transcribe on to a canvas correspond to something concrete, how can it be said that they lack a foundation in reality, do not form part of the real world? Also I'm attaching, as you can see, more and more importance to the objective content of my paintings.

It seems to me a prime necessity that there should be a strong and fruitful subject-matter that hits the spectator in the face before he can begin to collect his thoughts. This is poetry expressed in plastic terms and it speaks its own language. Under these conditions I can't understand—and I take it as an insult—when people include me with the abstract painters.

G. D. — If we draw a distinction between the pictures on the one hand which make do with empty space having no geometrical quality, pictures that are "lost" in a mathematical space inaccessible both to the senses and the heart, and those, on the other hand, which reveal the fluid, changeful, unforeseen phenomena of life—works that will make good in the future, in "the future's marvelous unknown"—it's a safe bet that we would not find many to place in the second category.

MIRÓ — Still, surely a canvas by Poussin or Seurat can't be compared to a working diagram. What affects us in Poussin is his prodigious mental élan; what delights us in Seurat is, combined with a sensibility at once refined and human in the broadest sense, his phantasmagorical, truly hallucinating vision of the world. In his work the sole use to which he puts his technical skill is that of bringing out the play of natural human forces.

G. D. — An expertness that often comes near to defeating them. A supremely gifted artist, Seurat spent a whole year on his *Poseuses*, strewing the canvas with thousands of complementary touches which, placed too near each other, grow blurred instead of standing out. And that ill-starred painter died when he was only thirty-two, worn out, we are told, by this singular activity.

MIRÓ — Anyhow expert technicians are less dangerous than *littérateurs*. These latter easily develop into the worst enemies of man, and they should be given short shrift, like the animals they are. I've come across men of that type who have the nerve to describe Van Gogh, that radiant soul, as a mere simpleton and to refer to those wonderful beings Cézanne and Rousseau, as "bunglers." What finer examples could you have of "intellectual" imbecility! Yes, one poet's worth a thousand *littérateurs*... And I don't draw any distinction between painting and poetry. I often "illustrate" my canvases with lines of poetry, and *vice versa*. Isn't this just what those *grands seigneurs* of the mind, the Chinese, used to do?

G. D. — To such an extent that they often covered up a master painting on a scroll with their pretty little tales. Poetry was by way of expelling painting. Some pointsman had switched the train on to the wrong line.

MIRÓ — What if he did? The only thing that matters is to lay bare one's soul; making poetry or painting is like making love. What happens is an exchange of blood, a total embrace—reckless and defenseless! Even those who refuse to fall under the spell of Picasso find an overwhelming significance in his work. His possible shortcomings, his vulnerable points, serve only to make us better understand his personality—which in any case is still too near for us to be able to discuss it.

G. D. — Picasso himself would ask us not only not to discuss painting but also not to try to grasp its meaning. On the other hand, he admits that the poet and the painter can on occasion be public dangers; allows, in fact, a certain scope for the presentment, in art, if not of "the beautiful and the ugly," of Good and Evil and other metaphysical speculations, anyhow as to what is good or bad. A simple question of hygiene!

MIRÓ — A question of personal experience. At a time when I felt terribly alone, Huysmans with his craving for revolt, his urge to escape, did me no end of good.

G. D. — Whereas to me he seems to have moved from the gutter into the holy-water stoup (after lingering among the antiquarians) by a strangely slow and devious route.

MIRÓ — And Roussel...

G. D. — On me he produces the effect of a dentist, his hands full of terrifying little instruments.

MIRÓ — Not on me! He gives me refreshing emotions. Eluard delights me with his fine precision. Bach...

G. D. — (Primordial clock-maker, God the Father's head mechanic!)

MIRÓ — ...gives me lessons in large-scale architecture. Mozart...

G. D. — (At last!)

MIRÓ — Mozart invites love—with his purity, with the generosity and simplicity of his love. All these men help one to live in this sordid world of today. And in the forefront of the men of genius I place Antonio Gaudi...

G. D. — ...who to your regret, I'm sure, did not rebuild the whole of Barcelona. It would have been child's play for me. What a town we'd then have had for our holidays! A living forest of symbols! I can picture in it octopus banks, slug schools, and shops like toads, all linked together by roads made of bits of broken crockery and cable-cars like winged dragons. From the itinerant cathedral, made of dry saliva, petrified sponges, clippings of hair, would spurt forth flood-lit cascades, while biblical heroes, attended by their favorite animals and moved by clockwork, fall to dancing a quadrille. Grave professors, nimble students, captains of industry done from nature, start singing in the trees at the top of their voices every time a ship is wrecked, fooled by the Bengal lights and revolving mirrors of the harbor. A mirage city (you said it!), a city scarred with eczema, a city of bogs and fens. How I'd have loved to see there, strolling hand in hand, exchanging becks and smiles, Messieurs Breton and Dali—on the days, of course, when they're not busy on the barricades!

MIRÓ — Tourists never appreciate Gaudi's genius. So deeply rooted are the misunderstandings between one country and another that it would be better if people gave up traveling. It breaks my heart to see a Catalan following in the footsteps of Claude Monet, grand though Monet is, and wanting to illustrate Mallarmé. Or when another of my friends, a Frenchman, rushes to Castile to find "effects of cruelty" and persists in illustrating Cervantes. What a hopeless, tragic muddle!

G. D. — So you think that everyone who travels carries his own lamp with him...

MIRÓ — And that everywhere one finds the sun, a blade of grass, the spirals of the dragon-fly. Courage consists in staying at home and close to Nature, Nature who takes no account of our calamities. Every grain of dust has a wonderful soul, but to understand it one needs to regain the religious, magic sense of things, the spirit of primitive peoples...

G. D. — ...which has enabled you to engage for a round tour of the two continents the king of the Gogotians and his suite, who normally dwell on the heights of Montserrat. You and your troupe set out, with all the scenery of winter and summer in your baggage, at the time of day when the sun bathes in brazen fervor the stone inquisitors, the swooning apes, the minister of Phalli, to which that ancient monastery owes its fame. So now the king opens for the first time his lidless eyes on the world of subways and *vernissages*, and his three hairs bristle with rage, he can't believe his eyes. But the ghouls, the elfs and cherubs make themselves invisible and continue their pranks. Naughty and perverse, like all children, they nibble at the moon, swing on wisps of cloud, conjure away the bullfinch, suck the cream of craters, smear themselves with blood, clothe themselves with snow and, with the loving care of Moslem calligraphers, trace on the fur of animals those cabalistic signs which make the genii of fire and air burst into song. Just so the sailors and peasants of your country have the gift of drawing in clever, smudgy lines upon the wood of their doors or the cement of urinals, amongst delightful harmonies of dirty pinks, blurred yellows, dubious grey emblems of Dionysus or the Crucified, most virile and unloveliest of men.

MIRÓ — Everywhere, always, the man of the people has the same impulses and he spontaneously creates things that are quite miraculous. Hence the appeal, for me, of those anonymous works, the art of common folk, graffiti and the like, in which gestures and expressions are caught on the wing. But one needs to have kept enough purity oneself to be capable of being moved. Lose touch with the people and you lose touch with yourself.

G. D. — Everybody knows that the inarticulate masses have much to give us. But what have we to give them in exchange?

MIRÓ — The worst thing we could do would be for us to place ourselves below the crowd and flatter it by telling it stupid, sordid anecdotes. Our present-day leaders, bastard offspring of politics and the arts, claim to regenerate the world, but actually they're on the way to poisoning our last sources of refreshment. Whether they talk of tradition and high ideals, or of revolution and a workers' paradise, we can see their little bellies sticking out and symptoms of fatty degeneration of the soul.

G. D. — The politician, worse luck, survives all shipwrecks. Like the stormy petrel he floats and gloats when others sink. We, I'm sure, could hit it off much better with the trade unions.

MIRÓ — Provided we're not asked to drag down the artist to the level of a community which, on the contrary, needs his uplift if it's to regain its dignity. Individualism, no doubt, is a sign of decadence. In all the great periods of history the individual and the group marched hand in hand. But today what's there to hope for? Personally I content myself, for the present, with registering images and sensations as accurately as I can, without any ulterior motive. What people say of these productions leaves me completely cold. The changes happening in my consciousness take place without my knowledge. I'm guided by what's happening in front of me (I realize this afterwards) and this obliges me to act as I do.

It's best not to attach importance to one's works. The less we aim at a fine success, the better our chance of bringing it off—of bringing off, I mean to say, a decent piece of work. After all, what gives rise to a picture is an overflow of emotions and sensations. It's a product of evacuation, to which one never returns.

G. D. —Here again you're in agreement with Picasso—but the word he uses is "indigestion." And Braque has the same view, I think. Juan Gris used to say he treated each composition as a theorem and, once it was proved, he turned his back on it. Just now, however, you spoke of love and the happy confidence it inspires. But there's more to it than a physical act; it's a living creature you're trying to bring to birth. If that's so, how can you take no further interest in your work, not want to know who joyfully adopts it and what use he makes of it?

MIRÓ — You asked that question, yourself: Where to go? Whom to cling to? If historical events are compulsive enough, we shall follow their lead, without even knowing it. Deliberately to join forces with them would be playing the dilettante.

G. D. — Before long you probably won't have the choice. Wherever you go you'll have to answer Yes or No to the demands of the rival parties, as was the case under the Athenian tyrant. Even admitting that these nation-wide mobilizations deprive us of much that's precious to us . . .

MIRÓ — Yes, here I'm pessimistic, tragically pessimistic. I've no illusions left. There's going to be a fight, even fiercer than in the past, against everything that stands for a purely spiritual value.

G. D. — "The Babes in the Wood." But don't let's take the prophets of gloom too seriously. There must be somewhere, amongst the trees, one of those hidden treasures that the "babes" will hit on just when, half dead of cold and hunger, they least expect it. And if the road seems to them too long, you can always point the way and teach them how, by simply raising a finger, one can transform ruins into castles, fairy castles built of flames, with people dancing around them, shouting for joy!

SELECT BIBLIOGRAPHY

Writings and Statements by Miró

Variétés, special issue on *Le Surréalisme en 1929*, Brussels, June 1929. — Statements quoted by Tériade, *Minotaure*, No. 3-4, December 1933. — Interview with Georges Duthuit, *Où allez-vous Miró?*, in *Cahiers d'Art*, No. 8-10, 1936. — *Je rêve d'un grand atelier*, in *XXe Siècle*, No. 2, May 1938. — *Le Carnaval d'Arlequin*, in *Verve*, No. 4, January-March 1939. — *Jeux poétiques*, in *Cahiers d'Art*, Vol. 20-21, 1945-1946. — J. J. SWEENEY, *Joan Miró, Comment and Interview*, in *Partisan Review*, February 1948. — *Cobalto*, No. 1, Barcelona 1949. — R. BERNIER, *Miró céramiste, interview par correspondance*, in *L'Œil*, No. 17, May 1956. — E. SCHEIDEGGER, *Joan Miró, Gesammelte Schriften*, Zurich 1957. — *Ma dernière œuvre est un mur*, in *Derrière le Miroir*, No. 107-109, Galerie Maeght, Paris 1958. — *Je travaille comme un jardinier*, in *XXe Siècle*, No. 1, February 15, 1959. — *Entretien radiophonique avec G. Charbonnier*, in *Le Monologue du Peintre*, Julliard, Paris 1960. — Statements in *Daedalus*, Vol. 89, No. 1, Cambridge 1960. — R. J. MOULIN, *Un quart d'heure avec Joan Miró* (on engraving), *Lettres Françaises*, April 1961. — Statements quoted by R. Bernier, *L'Œil*, No. 79-80, July-August 1961.

Books illustrated by Miró

L. HIRTZ (Lise DEHARME), *Il était une petite fée*, color stencils, Jeanne Bucher, Paris 1928. — T. TZARA, *L'arbre des voyageurs*, 4 lithographs, Ed. Montaigne, Paris 1930. — G. HUGNET, *Enfances*, 3 etchings, Cahiers d'Art, Paris 1933. — T. TZARA, *L'antitête*, 8 etchings, Bordas, Paris 1947-1948. — *Album 13*, 13 lithographs in black and white, Maeght, Paris 1948. — T. TZARA, *Parler seul*, color lithographs, Maeght, Paris 1948-1950. — J. CABRAL DE MELO, *J. Miró*, 3 color woodcuts, Ed. de l'Oc, Barcelona 1950. — R. CREVEL, *La Bague d'aurore*, 6 etchings, 5 of them colored, L. Broder, Paris 1958. — P. ELUARD, *A toute épreuve*, 80 color woodcuts, G. Cramer, Geneva 1958. — R. CHAR, *Nous avons*, 5 colored etchings, L. Broder, Paris 1959. — Y. BONNEFOY, *Anti-Platon*, 7 etchings, 5 of them colored, Maeght, Paris 1962. — A. DU BOUCHET, *La lumière de la lame*, 7 etchings, 5 of them colored, Maeght, Paris 1962. — J. DUPIN, *Saccades*, 7 etchings, 5 of them colored, Maeght, Paris 1962. — *Album 19*, text by R. Queneau, 19 lithographs, Maeght, Paris 1962.

Miró has engraved a number of frontispieces for volumes of poetry published by his friends and has made lithograph illustrations for many of the catalogues of his exhibitions.

General Works

A. BRETON, *Le Surréalisme et la peinture*, Gallimard, Paris 1928. — A. OZENFANT, *Art*, Budry, Paris 1928. — *Die Kunst des 20. Jahrhunderts*, edited by C. Einstein, Propylaen, Berlin 1931. — A. JAKOVSKY, *Six essais*, Povolosky, Paris 1933. — *Histoire de l'Art contemporain, La Peinture*, text by J. CASSOU, documentation by G. BAZIN, Alcan, Paris 1935. — A. BRETON and P. ELUARD, *Dictionnaire abrégé du Surréalisme*, Beaux-Arts, Paris 1938 — C. ZERVOS, *Histoire de l'Art contemporain*, Cahiers d'Art, Paris 1938. — M. NADEAU, *Histoire du Surréalisme*, 2 vols., Ed. du Seuil, Paris 1945-1948. — A. BRETON, *Le Surréalisme et la Peinture, suivi de Genèse et Perspective artistiques du Surréalisme et de fragments inédits*, Brentano, New York 1945. — B. DORIVAL, *Les étapes de la peinture contemporaine*, Vol. III, Gallimard, Paris 1946. — J. T. SOBY, *Contemporary Painters*, Museum of Modern Art, New York 1948. — P. ELUARD, *Voir*, Trois Collines, Geneva 1948. — G. MARCHIORI, *Pittura moderna in Europa*, Pozza, Venice 1950. — *History of Modern Painting*, Vol. III: *From Picasso to Surrealism*, text by J. LASSAIGNE, Skira, Geneva 1950. — C. ESTIENNE, *Poésie des formes et des couleurs*, XXᵉ Siècle, June 1951. — A. BRETON, *Entretiens 1913-1952*, Gallimard, Paris 1952. — J. LASSAIGNE, *Spanish Painting*, Vol. II, Skira, Geneva 1952. — M. RAYNAL, *Modern Painting*, Skira, Geneva 1953. — W. HAFTMANN, *Malerei im 20. Jahrhundert*, Prestel Verlag, Munich 1954. — A. BRETON, *Les Manifestes du Surréalisme*, Le Sagittaire, Paris 1955. — C. GIEDION-WELCKER, *Plastik des 20. Jahrhunderts*, Hatje, Stuttgart 1955. — C. RODRIGUEZ AGUILEIRA, *Antologia espanole de arte contemporáneo*, Barna, Barcelona 1955. — M. BRION, *L'Art abstrait*, Albin Michel, Paris 1956. — P. COURTHION, *L'Art indépendant*, Albin Michel, Paris 1958. — A. MASSON, *Entretiens avec G. Charbonnier*, preface by G. Limbour, Julliard, Paris 1958. — M. JEAN, *Histoire de la Peinture surréaliste*, Ed. du Seuil, Paris 1959. — H. READ, *A Concise History of Modern Painting*, Thames & Hudson, London 1959. — F. MOURLOT, *Les affiches originales des maîtres de l'Ecole de Paris*, Sauret, Monte Carlo 1959. — J. CASSOU, *Panorama des Arts plastiques contemporains*, Gallimard, Paris 1960. — C. GREENBERG, *Art and Culture: Critical Essays*, Beacon Press, Boston 1961. — P. WALDBERG, *Surrealism*, Skira, Geneva 1962.

Monographs

J. J. SWEENEY, *Joan Miró*, catalogue of the exhibition at the Museum of Modern Art, New York 1941. — M. LEIRIS, *Les gravures de Joan Miró*, Curt Valentin, New York 1947. — C. GREENBERG, *Joan Miró*, with a memoir by Ernest Hemingway, Quadrangle Press, New York 1948. — R. QUENEAU, *Joan Miró ou le poète préhistorique*, Skira, Geneva 1949. — A. CIRICI-PELLICER, *Miró y la imaginación*, Omega, Barcelona 1949. — J. E. CIRLOT, *Joan Miró*, Cobalto, Barcelona 1949. — J. CABRAL DE MELO,

Joan Miró, Ed. de l'Oc, Barcelona 1950. — F. ELGAR, *Miró*, Hazan, Paris 1954. — J. PREVERT and G. RIBEMONT-DESSAIGNES, *Joan Miró*, Maeght, Paris 1956. — A. VERDET, *Joan Miró*, photos by R. Hauert, Kister, Geneva 1956. — A.VERDET, *Joan Miró*, Galerie Matarasso, Nice 1957.— S. HUNTER, *Joan Miró, Das graphische Werk*, Hatje, Stuttgart 1958. — W. ERBEN, *Joan Miró*, Prestel Verlag, Munich 1959. — J. GOMIS and J. PRATS, *The Miró Atmosphere*, photos by Gomis, Wittenborn, New York 1959. — J. T. SOBY, *Joan Miró*, Museum of Modern Art, New York 1959. — G. WEELEN, *Miró*, 2 vols., Hazan, Paris 1961. — J. DUPIN, *Miró*, DuMont Schauberg, Cologne, and Flammarion, Paris 1961.

Detailed bibliographies will be found in the monographs by C. GREENBERG (by H. B. Muller), J. T. SOBY (by B. Karpel) and J. DUPIN (by B. Karpel).

Special Issues of Magazines

L'Amic de les Arts, No. 26, Sitges, June 1928, texts by M. A. Cassanyes, S. Dali, J. V. Foix, S. Gasch. — *Cahiers de Belgique*, June 1929, texts by S. Dali, R. Desnos, S. Gasch, W. George. — *Cahiers d'Art*, No. 1-4, 1934, texts by G. Antheil, R. Desnos, J. V. Foix, R. Gaffé, W. Grohmann, P. Guéguen, E. Hemingway, R. Hoppe, V. Huidobro, A. Jakovsky, L. Massine, B. Péret, H. Read, J. J. Sweeney, M. Raynal, J. Viot, C. Zervos. — *Gaceta de Arte*, No. 38, Teneriffe, June 1936, texts by E. Westerdahl, R. Hoppe, V Huidobro, L. Massine, C. Zervos. — *Cahiers d'Art*, Vol. 20-21, 1945-1946, works of 1944-1945 (50 plates), texts by Miró and T. Tzara. — *Derrière le Miroir*, No. 14-15, 1948, text by G. Limbour; No. 29-30, 1950, texts by M. Leiris, R. Queneau and J. Prévert; No. 57-59, 1953; No. 87-89, 1956, texts by J. L. Artigas, J. Prévert and G. Ribemont-Dessaignes; No. 117, 1959; No. 119, 1960; No. 120, 1960, texts by J. Prévert and R. Queneau; No. 123, 1961, text by J. Gardy Artigas; No. 128, 1961, texts by J. Prats and J. Brossa. — *Mizue*, No. 570, Tokyo 1953, text by G. Duthuit. — *Los papeles de Son Armadans*, No. XXI, Madrid-Palma de Mallorca, December 1957, texts by C. J. Cela, J. Cassou, V. Aleixandre, J. V. Foix, A. Kerrigan, C. E. Ferreiro, L. F. Vivanco, J. E. Cirlot, A. Crespo, B. Bonet, J. M. Caballero Bonald, E. Lafuente Ferrari, G. de Torre, R. Gullón, J. L. Artigas, R. Santos Torroella, E. Westerdahl, F. M. Lorda Alaiz.

Many references to Miró and his work will be found in *La Révolution surréaliste*, edited first by P. Naville and B. Péret, then by A. Breton, Paris 1925-1929, and in *Minotaure*, edited by Albert Skira, Paris 1933-1937.

Principal Magazine Articles

M. LEIRIS, *Joan Miró*, Little Review, New York, Spring-Summer 1926. — S. GASCH, *L'obra del pintor Joan Miró*, L'Amic de les Arts, No. 5, Sitges, August 1926. — J. de BOSCHÈRE, *Notes sur la peinture et Miró*, Variétés,

Brussels, July 15, 1928. — S. GASCH, *Joan Miró*, Gaseta de les Arts, Barcelona, March 1929. — W. GEORGE, *Miró et le miracle ressuscité*, Le Centaure, No. 8, Brussels, May 1, 1929. — M. LEIRIS, *Joan Miró*, Documents, No. 5, Paris 1929. — G. BATAILLE, *Joan Miró, peintures récentes*, Documents, No. 7, Paris 1930. — G. HUGNET, *Joan Miró ou l'enfance de l'art*, Cahiers d'Art, No. 7-8, Paris 1931. — J. J. SWEENEY, *Miró and Dali*, New Republic, New York, February 6, 1935. — M. HENRY, *Joan Miró*, Cahiers d'Art, No. 5-6, Paris 1935. — J. FREY, *Miró and the Surrealists*, Parnassus, New York, October 1936. — J. VIOT, *Un ami, Joan Miró*, Cahiers d'Art, No. 8-10, Paris 1936. — P. ELUARD, *Naissance de Miró*, Cahiers d'Art, No. 1-3, Paris 1937. — J. LARREA, *Miroir d'Espagne*, Cahiers d'Art, No. 4-5, Paris 1937. — G. L. K. MORRIS, *Miró and the Spanish Civil War*, Partisan Review, New York, February 1938. — L. VARGAS, *Joan Miró*, Konstrevy, No. 15, Stockholm 1939. — T. TZARA, *A propos de Joan Miró*, and G. HUGNET, *Poème*, Cahiers d'Art, No. 3-4, Paris 1940. — P. WATSON, *Joan Miró*, Horizon, No. 20, London, August 1941. — J. J. SWEENEY, *Joan Miró*, Ars, No. 5, Mexico City, May 1943. — J. J. SWEENEY, *Miro's Mirror Magic*, Town and Country, New York, April 1945. — P. GASSIER, *Miró et Artigas*, Labyrinthe, No. 22-23, Geneva, December 1946. — G. LIMBOUR, *Souvenirs sûr un peintre, Joan Miró*, Arts de France, No. 17-18, Paris 1947. — J. GOMEZ SICRE, *Joan Miró in New York*, Right Angle, No. 10, Washington, January 1948. — J. F. RAFOLS, *Miró antes de la Masia*, Anales y Boletin de los Museos de Arte de Barcelona, No. 1-2, 1948. — G. DORFLES, *Per Joan Miró*, Critica d'Arte, No. 4, Florence, November 1949. — C. ZERVOS, *Remarques sur les œuvres de Miró*, Cahiers d'Art, Vol. 24, Paris 1949. — R. SANTOS TORROELLA, *Joan Miró en su estudio*, Indice de las Artes, Madrid, February 1950. — J. J. SWEENEY, *Miró*, Art News, No. 7, New York November 1953. — P. COURTHION, *Jeu et fantaisie de Miró*, XXᵉ Siècle, No. 6, January 1956. — J. DUPIN, *Miró*, Quadrum, No. 2, Brussels, May 1956. — G. LIMBOUR, *Un nouveau Miró*, XXᵉ Siècle, No. 7, Paris, June 1956. — H. Weiss, *Miró — Magic with Rocks*, Art News, No. 4, New York, Summer 1956. — A. JOUFFROY, *Portrait d'un artiste, Joan Miró*, Arts, Paris, July 25, 1956. — P. GUÉGUEN, *L'humour féerique de Joan Miró*, XXᵉ Siècle, No. 8, Paris, January 1957. — D. ASHTON, *Miró-Artigas*, Craft Horizons, No. 1, New York, February 1957. — I. YANAIHARA, *Les céramiques de Miró*, Mizue, No. 620, Tokyo, March 1957. — P. GUÉGUEN, *J. L. Sert: L'atelier du peintre Miró à Palma de Majorque*, Aujourd'hui, No. 15, Paris, December 1957. — E. Roditi, *Entretien avec Joan Miró*, Arts, No. 1, New York, October 1958. — A. BRETON, *Constellations de Joan Miró*, L'Œil, No. 48, Paris, December 1958. — P. SCHNEIDER, *Miró*, Horizon, No. 4, New York, March 1959. — W. RUBIN, *Miró in Retrospect*, Art International, No. 5-6, Zurich 1959. — R. Motherwell, *Significance of Miró*, Art News, New York, May 1959. — J. J. SWEENEY, *Two Walls by Joan Miró*, Quadrum, No. 6, Brussels 1959. — D. VALLIER, *Avec Miró*, Cahiers d'Art, Vol. 33-35, Paris 1960.

MAJOR EXHIBITIONS

Collective Exhibitions:

1925, Paris, Galerie Pierre, *Surrealist Painting.* — 1930, Paris, Galerie Goemans, *Collages.* — 1932, Paris, Galerie Pierre Colle, *Surrealist Exhibition.* — 1935, Teneriffe, *Surrealist Exhibition.* — 1936, New York, Museum of Modern Art, *Fantastic Art, Dada, Surrealism.* — 1937, Tokyo, Japanese Salon, *International Exhibition.* — 1938, Paris, Galerie Beaux-Arts, *International Surrealist Exhibition.* — 1940, Mexico City, *International Surrealist Exhibition.* — 1941, Richmond, *The W. P. Chrysler Jr. Collection.* — 1942, New York, Museum of Modern Art, *Painting and Sculpture in the Museum of Modern Art.* — 1946, Boston, Institute of Contemporary Art, *Four Spaniards.* —1947, Paris, Galerie Maeght, *International Surrealist Exhibition.* — 1948, San Francisco Museum of Art, *The Spanish Masters of 20th-Century Painting.* — 1952, Saarbrücken, *Surrealist Painting in Europe.* — 1954, Philadelphia Museum of Art, *The Louise and Walter Arensberg Collection.* — 1955, Kassel, *Documenta I.* — 1958, Brussels, *Fifty Years of Modern Art.* — 1958, Liège, Musée, *Léger, Matisse, Picasso, Miró, Laurens, Magnelli, Arp, Hartung and Jacobsen.* — 1959, Kassel, *Documenta II.* — 1961, New York, Knoedler Gallery, *The J. T. Soby Collection.* — 1961, Boston, Museum of Fine Arts, *The Artists and the Book, 1860-1960.*

One-Man Shows:

1918, Barcelona, Dalmau Gallery. — 1921, Paris, Galerie La Licorne, preface by M. Raynal. — 1925, Paris, Galerie Pierre, preface by B. Péret. — 1928, Paris, Galerie Georges Bernheim. — 1929, Brussels, Galerie Le Centaure. — 1930, Paris, Galerie Pierre, papiers collés. — 1930, New York, Valentin Gallery. — 1931, Chicago, Arts Club. — 1931, Paris, Galerie Pierre, object-sculptures. — 1932, New York, Pierre Matisse Gallery, paintings on paper. — 1932, Paris, Galerie Pierre Colle. — 1933, Paris, Galerie G. Bernheim. — 1933, New York, Pierre Matisse Gallery. — 1934, Paris, Galerie des Cahiers d'Art, early works. — 1935, New York, Pierre Matisse Gallery, oil and tempera paintings and pastels. — 1936, New York, Pierre Matisse Gallery, retrospective. — 1937, London, Zwemmer Gallery. — 1938, New York, Pierre Matisse Gallery. — 1938, London, Mayor Gallery. — 1940, New York, Pierre Matisse Gallery. — 1941, New York, Museum of Modern Art, catalogue by J. J. Sweeney. — 1945, Paris, Galerie Vendôme, preface by L. PARROT. — 1947, New York, Pierre Matisse Gallery. — 1948, New York, Pierre Matisse Gallery. — 1948, Paris, Galerie Maeght, recent works. — 1949, Stockholm, Blanche Gallery, preface by R. Hoppe. — 1949, Bern, Kunsthalle. — 1949, Basel,

Kunsthalle. — 1950, Paris, Galerie Maeght. — 1950, Stockholm, Blanche Gallery, sculptures and graphic art. — 1951, New York, Pierre Matisse Gallery. — 1951, Milan, Galleria del Naviglio, preface by G. Dorfles. — 1953, Paris, Galerie Maeght. — 1953, New York, Pierre Matisse Gallery, preface by J. J. Sweeney. — 1954, Krefeld, Museum. — 1954, Venice, Biennale, preface by C. Estienne. — 1956, Brussels, Palais des Beaux-Arts, retrospective. — 1956, Basel, Kunsthalle, preface by A. Rüdlinger. — 1956, Paris, Galerie Maeght, ceramics. — 1956, New York, Pierre Matisse Gallery, ceramic sculptures. — 1957, New York, Pierre Matisse Gallery. — 1957, Krefeld, Museum, complete graphic work, catalogue by P. Wember, preface by W. Schmalenbach. — 1958, Paris, Galerie Berggruen, presentation of Eluard's poems, *A toute épreuve*, illustrated by Miró. — 1958, New York, Pierre Matisse Gallery, "peintures sauvages", preface de J. Fitzsimmons. — 1959, Paris, Galerie Berggruen, presentation of the album *Constellations*, published by Pierre Matisse. — 1959, Rome, Galleria Il Segno, graphic work. — 1960, New York, Museum of Modern Art, retrospective. — 1961, Barcelona, Sala Gaspar, ceramic mural for Harvard. — 1961, Paris, Galerie Maeght, recent paintings. — 1961, Paris, Galerie Maeght, mural paintings. — 1961, Geneva, Athénée, graphic work and ceramics, preface by M. Leiris. — 1961, New York, Pierre Matisse Gallery, preface by Y. Tallandier. — 1962, Paris, Musée d'Art Moderne, retrospective, preface by J. Cassou. — 1962, Tokyo, Museum of Western Art, graphic work. — 1963, London, Tate Gallery, retrospective. — 1966, Philadelphia Museum of Art, graphic work. — 1966, Tokyo, Museum of Modern Art, and Kyoto, Museum of Modern Art, retrospective. — 1968, Saint-Paul de Vence, Fondation Maeght, retrospective. — 1968-1969, Barcelona, Santa Creue, retrospective. — 1969, Munich, Haus der Kunst. — 1969, Barcelona, House of Architects, "Miró Otro". — 1969, New York, Museum of Modern Art, recent prints. — 1971, Knokke (Belgium), Casino.

BIBLIOGRAPHICAL SUPPLEMENT

J. Dupin, *Joan Miró. Life and Work*, New York 1962. — P. Kantor, *Drawings by Joan Miró*, New York 1962. — Y. Bonnefoy, *Miró*, Paris 1964, New York and London 1967. — W. Erben, *Joan Miró*, Monte Carlo 1964. — J. Dupin, *Joan Miró*, Paris 1967 and Boston 1970. — M. Tapié, *Joan Miró*, Paris and New York 1970. — R. Penrose, *Miró*, London and New York 1970. — M. Chilo, *Miró*, Boston 1971.

GENERAL INDEX

LIST OF COLORPLATES

CONTENTS

THIS VOLUME OF THE SERIES "THE TASTE OF OUR TIME"
WAS PRODUCED BY THE TECHNICAL STAFF OF EDITIONS
D'ART ALBERT SKIRA. FINISHED THE TWENTY-FIRST
DAY OF MARCH NINETEEN HUNDRED AND SEVENTY-TWO.

TEXT AND ILLUSTRATIONS BY

SKIRA

COLOR STUDIOS
AT IMPRIMERIES RÉUNIES S.A., LAUSANNE
AND PRESSES CENTRALES S.A., LAUSANNE

PLATES ENGRAVED BY GUEZELLE & RENOUARD, PARIS

PHOTOGRAPHS BY

*Louis Laniepce, Paris (pages 19, 25, 29, 32, 41, 44, 45, 47, 48, 49, 51, 52, 55,
59, 60, 64, 67, 70, 73, 86, 87, 92, 93, 100, 101, 105, 106, 108, 109, 111, 112,
115), Guezelle, Paris (page 83 and dustjacket), Henry B. Beville, Washington
(pages 23, 74, 80, 95), Umberto Rossi, Venice (page 57), Sandak, New York
(pages 30, 31, 56), and by courtesy of Mr Joaquim Gomis, Barcelona (page 14),
the Photographic Services of the Art Institute of Chicago (page 22) and DuMont
Schauberg Verlag, Cologne (page 26).*

PRINTED IN SWITZERLAND